GREAT QUARTERBACKS

GREAT QUARTERBACKS
FOOTBALL'S LEGENDARY LEADERS

GREG GARBER

MetroBooks

Dedication

To Gerry, Emily, and Christopher

Acknowledgments

The author would like to thank all the people who helped pull this book together, in no particular order: Don Smith of the Pro Football Hall of Fame; the public relations people of the NFL, especially Leslie Hammond; the league's great quarterbacks, in particular Phil Simms; Nathaniel Marunas for his diligent attention to matters editorial; and the helpful people and vast resources of ESPN.

MetroBooks

An Imprint of Friedman/Fairfax Publishers

© 1995 by Michael Friedman Publishing Group, Inc.

Library of Congress Cataloging-in-Publication Data

Garber, Angus G.
    Great quarterbacks: football's legendary leaders / Greg Garber.
    p. cm.
    Includes bibliographical references and index.
  ISBN 1-56799-169-6
  1. Football players—United States—Biography. 2. Quarterback (Football) I. Title.
  GV939.A1G37 1995
  796.332'092'2—dc20
  [B]

95-783
CIP

Editor: Nathaniel Marunas
Art Director: Jeff Batzli
Design: Smay Vision
Photography Editor: Wendy Missan

Color separations by Advance Laser Graphic Arts (International) Ltd.
Printed in China by Leefung-Asco Printers Ltd.

For bulk purchases and special sales, please contact:
Friedman/Fairfax Publishers
Attention: Sales Department
15 West 26th Street
New York, NY 10010
212/685-6610 FAX 212/685-1307

CONTENTS

INTRODUCTION

The most heralded class of college quarterbacks in history arrived in the National Football League in 1983. Stanford's John Elway, the number one pick overall, went to Baltimore. Todd Blackledge of Penn State, the number seven pick, went to Kansas City. The University of Miami's Jim Kelly, the number fourteen pick, went to Buffalo. Tony Eason of Indiana, the number fifteen pick, went to New England. Ken O'Brien of the University of California, Davis, the number twenty-four pick, went to the New York Jets. And the University of Pittsburgh's Dan Marino, the number twenty-seven pick, was snatched up by Miami. These young men were fully expected to become the best and the brightest professional quarterbacks ever.

More than a decade later, it is clear that they delivered on their enormous promise. "Yeah," says Kelly, who guided the Buffalo Bills to an unprecedented four consecutive Super Bowl appearances. "We did all right for ourselves, didn't we?"

Well, yes. Three of the Class of '83—Marino, Elway, and Kelly—seem destined for the Pro Football Hall of Fame. Elway and Marino insist that the competitive nature of playing as a contemporary of five other talented quarterbacks urged them to greater heights once they reached center stage in the NFL.

"You can't compare anything to 1983, because nothing before it and nothing after it can compare to that class," says Miami coach Don Shula. "I don't think anything will ever top it."

That's easy for him to say; Shula escaped with the steal of the draft. When unfounded rumors that Dan Marino was having trouble with drug use circulated around the league, the six-foot-four-inch, 224-pound Marino slipped to the bottom of the first round of the draft. The Dolphins, who had just reached the Super Bowl (and therefore had a low draft slot), were ecstatic to find him available.

Though Marino was the last of the six quarterbacks taken, he is likely to stand first in the NFL record books if he can stay healthy on the backside of his career. After the 1993 season, Marino already held more than twenty league records and was ranked among history's top three quarterbacks in the critical areas of pass attempts, completions, and touchdowns.

Marino holds the record for touchdown passes in a single season (48), set in 1984. What's the second-highest total? Marino's 44, accomplished in 1986. George Blanda and Y.A. Tittle are tied for history's third-best total, a relatively paltry 36 touchdown passes.

In his first ten seasons, Marino led the league in completions a record-tying five times. Sammy Baugh, the man whose record he equaled, needed twelve seasons to post that mark.

In 1984, Marino became the only man to pass for more than 5,000 yards (5,084, to be exact) in a season. His 4,746 in 1986 is the third-highest total ever. In 1984, Marino passed for more than 400 yards in a game a staggering four times. In 1986, he managed the feat three times. What is history's next best total? Marino and ten others—including Joe Montana and Dan Fouts (who did it twice each)—managed to pass for 400-plus yards twice in a season.

What is Marino's greatest strength? "He has a lightning-quick release," says no less an authority than Elway. "You just can't get to him."

The same, of course, is true of John Elway. And of the Gang of Six, he has the biggest heart. While he was never blessed with a wide-open offensive system (such as

After the 1994 season, Miami quarterback Dan Marino was already closing in on the most important quarterback records; he had completed 3,604 of 6,049 passes for 45,173 yards and 328 touchdowns.

Shula's, for instance) in Denver, Elway nevertheless maintains the best winning percentage of the Class of '83.

Elway was the first pick of the 1983 draft, but was traded a week later from Baltimore (which was not *his* first choice) to Denver (where he wanted to play). Elway's specialty is the two-minute drill, when the game hangs in the balance and the Broncos need points. He has led an incredible 32 fourth-quarter game-saving drives. "He is," Kelly says, "the classic clutch player."

Jim Kelly eschewed the NFL for the rival United States Football League and over two seasons produced statistics that bordered on the surreal. Kelly completed 63 percent of his passes for the Houston Gamblers, throwing for 9,842 yards and 83 touchdowns.

Kelly's arrival in Buffalo in 1986 signaled the beginning of the slow and steady rise of the Bills to the

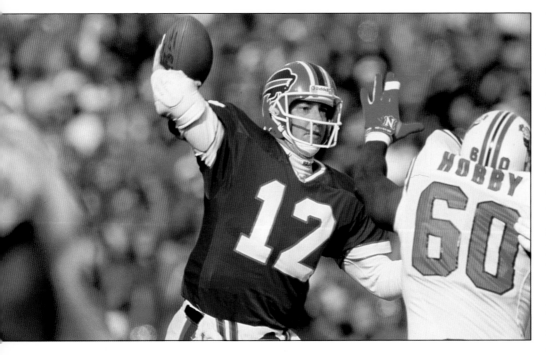

While Buffalo's Jim Kelly is probably best known for appearing in—and losing—four straight Super Bowls, he is also history's fifth-highest-ranked passer.

top of the American Football Conference. After eight seasons Kelly is history's fifth-highest-rated passer, based on the league's complicated formula.

Todd Blackledge was the only member of the Class of '83 to win a national college championship, but in seven seasons with Kansas City and Pittsburgh he made

only 29 starts. "My feeling about my career is that there is a great sense of incompleteness," says Blackledge, now a television analyst. "The fact that I can turn on the TV and see John playing and Danny playing and Jim...that part of it is difficult."

Tony Eason was 29-24 as a starter over eight seasons; in his final two years (spent with the Jets), he lived with his good friend Ken O'Brien. Although O'Brien's starting record was under .500, he remains the seventeenth-highest-rated passer of all time.

One statistic haunts the members of the Class of '83. "Until we win the big one, there's always going to be an asterisk next to us," Marino says.

Naturally, the "big one" is the Super Bowl. And the Class of '83 has a combined record of 0-9 in that department. Kelly is 0-4, Elway is 0-3, and Marino and Eason are each 0-1. Why?

"When six quarterbacks were drafted in the first round, it looked like it was going to make the AFC the conference of the future," says leading NFL analyst John Madden. "But I think the AFC relied too much on that. It became a passing conference and a pass-defense conference, and it wasn't as physical.

"The AFC didn't develop the strong running games and the big, strong offensive linemen and the tough defenses. The NFC didn't get the quarterbacks, so it had to rely on running backs and the running game. So instead of the Elways and Marinos winning the Super Bowl, it was guys like Mark Rypien, Phil Simms, Doug Williams, and Jim McMahon."

Says Elway, "I want as many shots at the Super Bowl as I can get. You'll never know what it's like to be a world champ unless you try. But if I don't win one, I can walk out and say, 'John Elway did everything he possibly could to win a Super Bowl.'"

"There's three of us left," Kelly says, "and one of us is going to get it."

"I'd definitely like to break the string," says Elway. Says Kelly, "It's just who gets there first."

"Hopefully," says Marino, "this year it will be me."

Though he wasn't always sur-
rounded by the best talent,
Denver's John Elway is the quintessential leader on the field.

ON THE BALL

So, what exactly does the quarterback do?

"What doesn't he do?" asks Hall of Famer Dan Fouts. "At times, the quarterback does a little of everything. He is all things to all people."

The quarterback receives the snap from center on virtually every offensive play, and in the span of three seconds he must decide which teammate will have the honor of trying to advance the ball. Even with the coaches on the sidelines calling the bulk of the plays, it is the quarterback who must execute the assignments and, quite often, change a play when the defense has correctly anticipated the offensive strategy with a formation that is sure to doom the original play.

The quarterback has to do all this with 300-pound defensive ends hurtling all around him and blitzing outside linebackers trying to squash him like a bug. It is because of the central role they play that quarterbacks make the million-dollar salaries and are the darlings of the media.

A quarterback must be tough and charismatic. He must be able to convince the men in his huddle time after time that they are better than they really are. He must be acutely aware of his team's personnel. He must understand the blocking assignments of each player, the pass routes, and the wide variety of options that can be invoked, depending on the defense. In short, he must manage the game, all the while working the clock as it winds down—seconds can mean the difference between winning and losing.

Dallas quarterback Troy Aikman has all the physical tools to succeed in the NFL, but it is his mental approach that wins games for the Cowboys.

"The way I prepare for a game is unlike any other player on offense," says Dallas Cowboys quarterback Troy Aikman. "The quarterback position is so much different than any other position on the field. I have to know the calls, the reads, what the receivers are doing on routes, what our [blocking] protection is. The other guys just have to know what they're doing, and that's it."

Aikman spends many hours each week studying videotapes of other teams for weaknesses in an opponent's game plan. He looks for defensive tendencies and personnel weaknesses he and his teammates can exploit. He has memorized his weekly custom-designed playbook for reads, keys, formations, pass routes, blocking schemes, audibles, and other options. He has learned the complex coded signals that will be relayed to him from the sidelines.

Roger Staubach, who presided over the original America's Team, says this of Aikman: "He's bigger than me, richer than me, and better-looking, too. Not to mention younger. Still, he's mature beyond his age as far as the position of quarterback goes. He's got the mental part down. He's in control.

"Physically," Staubach continues, "he can throw the heck out of the ball. But a lot of guys can do that. To have that balance out there, to be calm and know what you're doing, that's important."

Hugh Millen won a Super Bowl ring in 1993 with the Dallas Cowboys (he had been traded by the New England Patriots), where he backed up Aikman. His understanding of the duties of the quarterback and of the game is profound. "My job," Millen says, "is to deliver the football down the field. There are hazardous elements to that occupation. That's something you have to play with. Once you get to this level, most of the quarterbacks are able to deal with that. There are a lot of sixteen-year-old kids who look real good throwing a football in a park. But you put them in a high school football game and that's a different story. The ones who can't function in the pocket are weeded out at that point. And that weeding-out process continues, so by the time a quarterback gets to this level he's able to work effectively under duress."

There is another, seemingly menial task that falls to quarterbacks: taking the snap from center for field goals and point-after conversions. Some quarterbacks, like Jeff Rutledge, made a living holding for kicks. Rutledge won a national championship at the University of Alabama, but never made it as a regular starting NFL quarterback. Nonetheless, he extended his career for a handful of years with his unique talent.

In 1991 Rutledge scooped up a bad snap by John Brandes during a Monday Night Football game, enabling Washington Redskins placekicker Chip Lohmiller to boot a 52-yard field goal—Rutledge's presence of mind had earned him fifteen minutes of fame. ABC showed the play from several angles, and it appeared that Rutledge had made a near-miraculous play.

Rutledge didn't think the play was so miraculous. "I made ten or fifteen like that one over the years," Rutledge says. "One like that wasn't so tough because the AstroTurf made it easier to handle. It bounced right to me and I was able to get it down....

"It's not the hardest job in the world, but I don't think it's as easy as it looks. It's also one of those thankless jobs. Basically, all the holder can do is screw up."

HISTORY'S HANDOFFS

For every great moment in NFL history, there was probably a quarterback not too far away. Someone (Joe Ferguson) handed the ball off to O.J. Simpson when the Juice gained the last 7 of a record-setting 2,003 yards rushing on the final day of the 1973 season. Someone (Joe Montana) delivered the dramatic pass to receiver Dwight "The Catch" Clark that gave birth to the dynasty of the San Francisco 49ers. Someone (Jim McMahon) handed Walter Payton the ball when Payton surpassed Jim Brown to set the all-time rushing record in 1984.

The game's two greatest advances in the mind of the sporting public can be credited to two radically different quarterbacks, born a decade apart in Pennsylvania: Johnny Unitas and Joe Namath.

Johnny Unitas was the model of consistency during his career. Over a 47-game stretch between 1956 and 1960, he threw at least one touchdown pass each time he suited up.

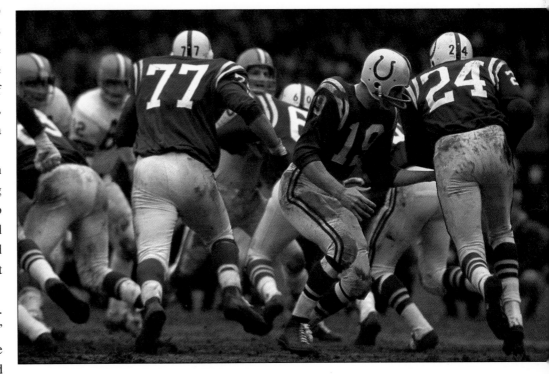

Believe it or not, there was a time when the NFL did not grip the United States with anything resembling passion. When the Baltimore Colts met the New York Giants in the 1958 championship game, football had

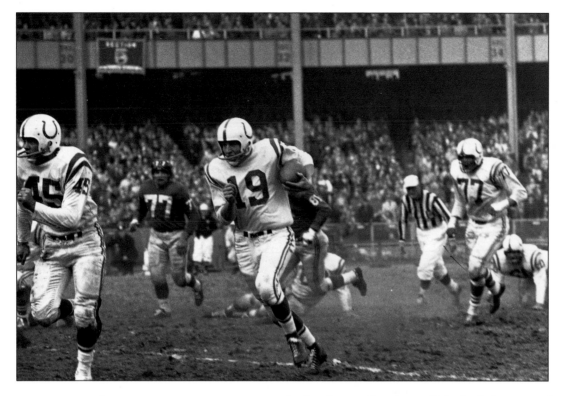 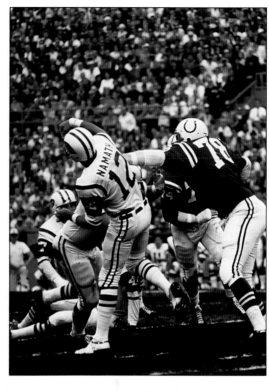

ABOVE: **It was Johnny Unitas who drove the Baltimore Colts to victory against the New York Giants in the celebrated 1958 NFL Championship Game.**

ABOVE RIGHT: **Eleven years later, Joe Namath carried the New York Jets to victory over the Colts in Super Bowl III.**

OPPOSITE: **Joe Montana was so cool in the pocket for the San Francisco 49ers that he almost seemed *devoid* of style. His precision and presence of mind allowed him to win all four of the Super Bowls he played in.**

crept past professional wrestling but still lacked the credibility of baseball, the national pastime. Johnny Unitas helped change all that.

Unitas was a scrappy 145-pound quarterback when the Pittsburgh Steelers drafted him in the ninth round of the 1955 draft. But when he was released without the honor of throwing a pass in a regular season game, the local semiprofessional team, the Bloomfield Rams, snapped him up. They paid him six dollars per game. A year later, on the advice of a Bloomfield fan, Colts coach Weeb Ewbank invited Unitas to training camp and ultimately offered him a seven-thousand-dollar contract.

By 1958, Unitas was the star of the Colts—his Most Valuable Player performance carried Baltimore to the league championship that season. The title game was the scene of unprecedented drama. The Giants led 17-14 with two minutes remaining, but Unitas drove the Colts from their own 14 yard line into field goal range. The successful field goal kick forced overtime, a first for the title game. Unitas crafted an 80-yard touchdown drive

to win the game, punctuated by Alan Ameche's 1-yard touchdown run.

The game became known as "The Greatest Game Ever Played" and converted millions to the game. Refrigerators were no longer safe during the halftime periods of nationally televised games.

Seven years later, when the established NFL and the relatively young American Football League were waging a bitter battle for the U.S. entertainment dollar, University of Alabama quarterback Joe Namath signed a $400,000 contract with the New York Jets. It was the most lucrative professional football contract ever offered and it gave the junior league a new credibility.

Eighteen months later, the merger between the AFL and NFL was sealed, and history gives Namath much of the credit. It was Namath, playing for Ewbank, who fittingly validated the merger on January 12, 1969, when the Jets upset the Colts in Super Bowl III. The stunning victory followed two Super Bowls that had featured relatively easy wins by the Green Bay Packers over inferior AFL teams.

Broadway Joe's magnetic personality, his memorable pregame guarantee of victory, and his on-field performance helped shift the balance of power among the teams of the newly merged league, signaling a new era in which football enjoyed unbridled popularity.

THE STYLE SPECTRUM

One style does not fit all quarterbacks. Hall of Fame quarterbacks come in all shapes, sizes, and temperaments. Namath was a flamboyant six-foot-two-inch, 200-pound signal-caller with a blindingly quick release. Of course, he also had two of history's most troublesome knees (both of which have been reconstructed a few times over the years). Fran Tarkenton was a five-foot-ten-inch, 180-pound scrambler whose healthy knees bought him enough time to become the most prolific passer (6,467 attempts, 3,686 completions, 47,003 yards) in history.

George Blanda played in four different decades, appearing in a total of 340 games over twenty-six seasons. He was forty-eight years old when he finally retired. Otto Graham played for only ten seasons, but like Blanda, he is in the Hall of Fame.

The Washington Redskins' Sammy Baugh was a world-class athlete who could punt the ball out of sight; Bob Griese of the Miami Dolphins actually wore eyeglasses.

Joe Montana, at six feet one inch and 190 pounds, looked fragile—even spindly—but his composure in the huddle and in the pocket made him one of the best quarterbacks who ever played the game.

"As you watch a game on TV, the athleticism of a John Elway or Dan Marino jumps out at you," Millen explains. "Montana, on the other hand, doesn't have a rocket arm. But his accuracy and timing are unmatched; so is his ability to anticipate what the defense is going to give him. I can't recall anybody who's ever been better.

"He's been in four Super Bowls and in each one he's been matched up against great quarterbacks [Ken Anderson, Dan Marino, Boomer Esiason, John Elway] who have had stellar years. But the Super Bowl really

reduced those quarterbacks in terms of their efficiency. It looked so dificult for them just to get a first down. Montana made it look so easy, and that's a credit to him."

Passing was Montana's forte in San Francisco. In contrast, his 49ers replacement, Steve Young, is more of a runner. Both Young and Randall Cunningham, quarterback for Philadelphia, echo the scrambling footsteps of Tarkenton. They may be the most gifted running quarterbacks ever to play the game.

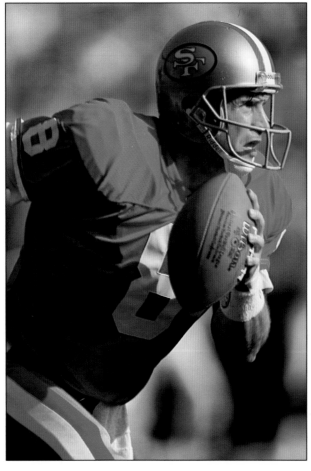

Steve Young was always a scrambler, beginning early in his NFL career with the Tampa Bay Buccaneers; but when he joined the San Francisco 49ers in 1987, his remarkable throwing arm was also showcased.

"Tarkenton was great to watch. He was smart and he reacted quickly when things were breaking down around him," says Giants owner Wellington Mara, whose team employed Tarkenton from 1967 to 1971. "But I don't think he is like Young or Cunningham. Cunningham is sensational. We never thought he would be the passer he has become. I know before the guy injured his knee he

ran without fear. There wasn't anything he couldn't do. The best pure passer I ever saw was Sammy Baugh, but he couldn't run like these guys."

Jim Finks, the late general manager of the New Orleans Saints, always maintained there were two types of running quarterbacks: pure runners and scramblers. "Tarkenton and [Roger] Staubach were guys that ran away from trouble, not by design. When they ran, they were buying more time, looking for something to develop downfield in the passing game.

"Young and Cunningham are pure runners. Young is as good as any I've ever seen. He can run inside. He can run outside. He can make you miss. Cunningham might be a little faster, but he can't make tacklers miss the way Young does."

Art Modell, the longtime Cleveland Browns owner, says, "I think you have to rank both Young and Cunningham right at the top. Let's face it, the defenses today are better. Everyone on the field defensively is bigger and faster than they were ten, twenty years ago.

"I think it's much tougher to be a great runner today than in the past because of the speed of the defense. For this reason, I like Young and Cunningham. They both have great speed. Young does some things that border on the miraculous. He runs like a running back. He makes people miss."

Bernie Kosar was never much on style; all he did was win. He graduated from the University of Miami in three years and found almost immediate success in the NFL. He had an ungainly sidearm delivery and his foot speed—well, foot speed would be an oxymoron. Still, he was able to avoid the pass rush when he had to.

"I've always felt I've been able to move around a little bit in the pocket to buy an extra split second or so to try to make some plays," Kosar says.

"People will always ridicule him for his lack of athletic ability," says Cleveland Browns head coach Bill Belichick, who eventually released Kosar in 1993. "But he can throw it to the right guy, and that's the main criteria for playing that position."

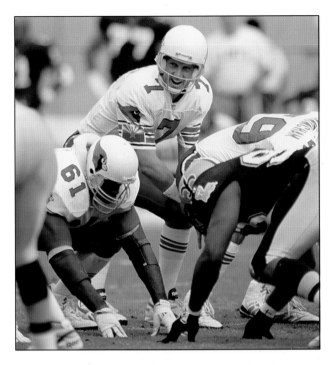

A RUN ON QUARTERBACKS

When the brave new world of free agency dawned on the NFL in 1993, running backs and strong safeties were not the main focus of the talent search—quarterbacks were. No fewer than sixteen notable quarterbacks changed teams, earning unprecedented money. Montana sparked controversy by leaving San Francisco, where he had won four Super Bowl rings, for a new life in Kansas City. Despite playing with a delicate hamstring, Montana led the Chiefs to the playoffs.

Jim McMahon, formerly a backup in Philadelphia behind Cunningham, signed with the Minnesota Vikings and carried them to the playoffs. Jeff Hostetler, who had played for years as the backup to Phil Simms, left the New York Giants and lifted the Los Angeles Raiders into postseason play. Steve Beuerlein moved out of the shadow of Aikman in Dallas to help the Phoenix Cardinals make a run at the playoffs. Bubby Brister left the Pittsburgh Steelers and almost elevated the Philadelphia Eagles into the playoffs.

In 1994 the competition reached a new level. Jim Everett was traded to the New Orleans Saints by the Los Angeles Rams. The Rams signed Atlanta's Chris Miller as a free agent. To fill the void that Miller's departure left, the Falcons convinced the Indianapolis Colts to deal them Jeff George.

Scott Mitchell left a comfortable position in Miami as Dan Marino's backup and accepted the starting job of the Detroit Lions. Chicago, in turn, hired Erik Kramer away from their division rivals in Detroit. Warren Moon, who made his reputation in Houston, was 1994's Jim McMahon in Minnesota.

McMahon, meanwhile, went back to the anonymity of a backup position. His goal? To last as long as Steve DeBerg, the posterboy of backup quarterbacks. DeBerg was drafted in the tenth round of the 1977 draft by the Dallas Cowboys. As his career progressed, it became clear his luck was terrible. Here, in order, are the first five quarterbacks he played behind: Roger Staubach, Joe Montana, John Elway, Steve Young, and Vinny Testaverde. Four of these five are either in the Hall of Fame or destined for enshrinement.

When DeBerg finally got a starting shot in Kansas City in 1990, he led the Chiefs to the playoffs—at the age of thirty-six. DeBerg threw 23 touchdown passes and was intercepted just 4 times in 444 attempts, good for the second-lowest interception rate in league history.

"The one thing I keep asking myself," DeBerg mused at the time, "is why couldn't all this have happened when I was still good?"

In 1993 history repeated itself, and DeBerg found himself playing behind another future Hall of Famer—Marino—when Marino and backup Scott Mitchell were hurt and DeBerg, at the age of thirty-nine, was asked to lead the Dolphins.

"Steve is intelligent and he's been around," explained Shula. "Quarterback is the one position where speed and agility aren't the essential tools. Knowing where to throw the ball is almost as important as getting it there."

"What goes around, comes around," said DeBerg. "You've heard the joke, right? Old quarterbacks don't die, they just fade back—to pass."

Steve Beuerlein produced modest numbers in Dallas before free agency came to the NFL in 1993. The Phoenix Cardinals quickly made him a Million Dollar Man.

CHAPTER ONE

THE TWO-MINUTE DRILL

There are certain plays in football that are reflex actions that result when certain conditions arise. For example, when a team is trying to come from behind, a loose, bend-but-don't-break prevent defense is deployed. Likewise, an offensive team desperate for points is expected to go into its two-minute drill—a hurry-up blur of activity designed to gain maximum yardage in minimum time.

Sometimes, however, the traditional ways do not apply; on rare occasions, genius springs from disaster. Consider the 1987 Buffalo Bills.

It was Marv Levy's first full year as head coach, and the Bills, coming off a 4-12 season, weren't destined for greatness that season. And yet, on September 20, quarterback Jim Kelly used the two-minute offense to lead the team to touchdowns in its final possessions. Buffalo beat the Houston Oilers 34-30, and a seed had been planted in the fertile minds of Buffalo's coaches. The Bills finished the season with a respectable record of 7-8, fourth in the American Football Conference Eastern Division.

By 1989 the Bills had risen to the top of the Eastern Division. The record was 12-4 in 1988 and 9-7 a year later. The Bills won games by scoring on their final 2 possessions with Kelly operating the no-huddle, hurry-up offense three times in 1989.

Buffalo offensive coordinator Ted Marchibroda had been around football for thirty years. As a quarterback himself at St. Bonaventure and the University of Detroit, Marchibroda was fascinated by the concept of a perpetual two-minute drill.

The Buffalo Bills' influential no-huddle offense began as a clutch play, but gradually Jim Kelly *(THIS PAGE AND OPPOSITE)* became the master of regular-play, no-huddle improvisation. Using the hurry-up offense, the Bills took the ball and made it all the way to appearances in an unprecedented four consecutive Super Bowls.

"Why," Marchibroda asked Levy one day after the 1989 season, "don't we use the hurry-up all the time?"

"That," Levy answered, "is a good question."

As radical a thought as it was, the no-huddle offense made a fair amount of sense. One of Kelly's gifts was his ability to assess a situation; he was the league's only quarterback allowed to call his own plays, and he had a knack for reading defenses on the fly. He also had one of the best complementary offenses in football, with wide receiver Andre Reed, multipurpose running back Thurman Thomas, and a vastly talented offensive line.

Jim Kelly and the Bills used their version of the two-minute drill down the stretch of the 1990 season and converted many cynics by scoring 95 points in 2 playoff games.

The Bills rarely made substitutions on offense, and Marchibroda knew if Kelly and company had the stamina to go without huddles and fire off plays with only ten-second intervals, the Bills could create an enormous advantage for themselves. By calling out plays and formations to his teammates at the line of scrimmage between snaps, Kelly prevented opponents from bringing in defensive specialists from the sidelines. This created favorable matchups for the Bills and left the eleven defenders gasping for breath. And unlike the trendy run-and-shoot offense, the Bills' no-huddle employed a tight end, the result being a highly credible running game. In fact, the Bills wound up throwing the ball only 60 percent of the time.

"I love being the guy who has to get it done," Kelly says. "Little League, high school football, even high school basketball, I've always been that way. Every game just seemed to wind up in my hands. If I made the big plays we were usually very successful; if I didn't, we usually lost. And that's what I like best about the no-huddle. Whether we score points or not, it's in my hands."

In 1990 the Bills first unveiled the no-huddle offense in some full-time sequences. After sporadic use during the season, they went to it exclusively in Game 11, against the Philadelphia Eagles. That day Buffalo scored 24 first-quarter points on the way to a 30-23 victory.

Not surprisingly, the Bills led the NFL with 428 points scored, a team record for regular-season points. Kelly was the league's top-rated passer (101.2) and Thomas led all runners for the second consecutive season with 1,829 combined yards. Reed caught 71 passes for 945 yards and 8 touchdowns.

In the rough-and-tumble playoffs, the no-huddle converted many of the league's cynics. In their first 2 games, the Bills scored an amazing 95 points and gained 995 yards. Those numbers are not misprints. The game that carried Buffalo to its first Super Bowl ever was a searing 51-3 victory over the Los Angeles Raiders in what was supposed to be a competitive AFC Championship Game. Only 2 playoff games in NFL history were won by wider margins.

"I'm telling you," said Howie Long, the Raiders' disconsolate defensive end, "I don't think anyone can stop it."

The Bills set an NFL record by scoring 41 points in the first half. When the Raiders switched to six defensive backs in the second quarter, the Bills ran the ball on 11 consecutive plays on the way to their third touchdown. Thomas, the embodiment of versatility, came away with 202 total yards. When the Raiders had one safety on the defensive line, the Bills ran outside. When the Raiders had two safeties, the Bills ran inside.

Levy, a man with a Harvard degree, downplayed the hybrid two-minute drill. "We haven't invented the Salk vaccine," the coach said. "It's just players playing together and getting better at it."

After the season ended, after the New York Giants had put an end to the Bills' marvelous run through the playoffs with a scintillating 20-19 victory in Super Bowl XXV, Marchibroda said he suspected that the rest of the league would soon catch up to the no-huddle. "One thing that helped us a lot last season was the surprise aspect of the no-huddle," Marchibroda said. "And we spoiled a lot of people with it. We're not going to go out and score 40 points every time."

In 1991, however, the Bills raised the no-huddle to an art form. Even the teams that had an entire off-season to prepare for Kelly's deadly scheme were humiliated. The Miami Dolphins succumbed in the opener (35-31) and the Pittsburgh Steelers were blinded (52-34) the following week. And so it went. By season's end, Buffalo had scored 458 points, another team record.

The no-huddle offense took the Bills to a record four consecutive Super Bowls. And despite their four losses to powerful NFC teams, the no-huddle may carry Kelly to the Pro Football Hall of Fame.

In the NFL, where everyone scrambles after the flavor of the month, most teams today have a version of the no-huddle that can be used at any time. The no-huddle has been called cutting-edge technology, a trend-setting device in a static league. But it merely proves, in an age of liberal player substitution and high-tech communications equipment, that there is nothing new under the sun when it comes to getting the ball into the end zone.

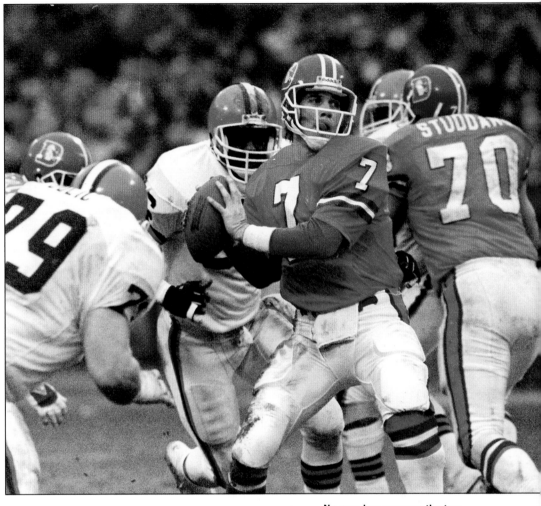

THE COMEBACK KID

The two-minute drill has been a football tradition for decades. Coaches devote a great deal of practice time to it because, statistically speaking, so many games are within reach as the clock winds down. The sum of the quarterback's skills are called on in a two-minute drill: physical gifts, judgment, resourcefulness, guts, time management. The good quarterback manages to raise the level of his game, while others around him shrink back from the pressure.

Producing impressive conventional statistics has never been the forte of John Albert Elway. Heading into the second decade of his celebrated career in 1993, his touchdown total of 158 was only 1 greater than his inter-

No man has ever run the two-minute drill better than Denver's John Elway. He has the rare combination of physical and mental skills to lift a team beyond its capabilities when the game is on the line. Here, he defeats the Cleveland Browns 23-20 in the overtime period of the 1986 AFC Championship Game.

ception total. The passer rating, which is used to measure a quarterback's skills, places great emphasis on efficiency but sometimes fails to recognize a bold quarterback who takes chances. Elway's mediocre passer rating reflects the limitations of the statistic.

Football's personnel analysts know, however, that numbers cannot measure a player's heart. That is why Elway was the first overall pick in the 1983 draft, ahead of such leading lights as Dan Marino and Jim Kelly.

The Denver Broncos had a spectacular 89-46-1 regular-season record in Elway's first decade. Denver was the American Football Conference representative in the Super Bowl in three of four seasons in the late 1980s, and Elway was the primary reason. The supporting cast on offense was thin and the defense lacked the physical gifts of some other teams, but Elway usually managed to move the Broncos down the field when points were needed.

And while other quarterbacks—notably, Joe Montana and Dan Marino—own many of the league's records in the areas of passer rating, yards, completions, touchdowns, and so on, Elway has a single statistic that money cannot buy. The magic number is 32—as in 32 fourth-quarter game-saving drives.

"I don't necessarily think he's the best quarterback in the NFL—I think he's the best player," says Denver owner Pat Bowlen. "If we were playing sandlot football out here, and all the players in the league were here, I'd take John first."

In his first eleven seasons, through 1993, Elway engineered 25 game-winning drives in the final fifteen minutes of a game—3 with less than three minutes left in the game, 14 with less than two minutes remaining, and 8 with less than one minute left. Elway was also responsible for 7 fourth-quarter game-tying drives; Denver went on to win 6 of those games and tie the remaining 1.

"We were always scrambling to catch up to teams," Elway says. "You sort of get into that two-minute mode, where you've got to get it done. It's something I've gotten used to over the years. Sure, I'm

ABOVE: The complicated passer rating system was not designed with John Elway in mind; his efforts to make things happen sometimes result in excessive interceptions.

OPPOSITE: Elway, letting it fly here against the Los Angeles Raiders, is a sure bet for the Pro Football Hall of Fame in Canton, Ohio.

Roger Staubach was, in many ways, the on-field version of Dallas Cowboys coach Tom Landry: cool and cerebral. Even under duress, Staubach performed with rare grace.

proud of it, but that's the quarterback's job—getting the ball down the field."

Says former Denver coach Dan Reeves, "John Elway has the ability to bring a team back, even when it looks like the game is over. He runs the two-minute drill as well as anyone."

THE ARTFUL DODGER

Reeves knows what he's talking about. Reeves played with and later coached Roger Staubach when the two were employed by the Dallas Cowboys. Staubach is considered to be the modern-day father of the two-minute drill.

In a Hall of Fame career shortened by service in the Navy, Staubach led the Cowboys to no fewer than 23 fourth-quarter come-from-behind victories. In total, fourteen of those comebacks were recorded in the final two minutes of a game or in overtime.

In 1972 Staubach authored his most famous comeback. Dallas trailed the San Francisco 49ers 28-13 in a playoff game, and Staubach was called from the bench to replace starting quarterback Craig Morton. Staubach had appeared in only 4 games that season because of a pre-season shoulder injury and had only 20 passes to his credit when he entered the game in the fourth quarter.

With seventy-eight seconds left, Dallas trailed 28-16, but Staubach took control of the game. A 20-yard touchdown pass to Billy Parks finished a 55-yard drive, tightening the score to 28-23. On the subsequent kickoff, Dallas placekicker Toni Fritsch successfully executed an onside kick, which the Cowboys recovered, giving them the ball again. Three plays later, the last a 10-yard touchdown pass to Ron Sellers, the Cowboys were 30-28 winners.

In 1975 Staubach led Dallas to an overtime win against the St. Louis Cardinals, produced 10 points in sixty-four seconds to defeat Philadelphia, and then stunned the Minnesota Vikings in a first-round playoff game with a 50-yard scoring pass to Drew Pearson as the clock ran down.

"He is," says former Dallas coach Tom Landry, "the greatest competitor I have ever seen."

Appropriately, Staubach's final regular-season game in 1979 featured a phenomenal comeback. He threw 2 touchdown passes in the final 140 seconds to defeat the rival Washington Redskins 35-34. Staubach's final regular-season pass was a 7-yard touchdown to Tony Hill. It came with thirty-nine seconds left in the game.

Roger Staubach, seen here under center against the San Francisco 49ers, was the architect of some of history's great finishes.

CHAPTER TWO

THE LEADER

Again and again, Joe Montana *(THIS PAGE AND OPPOSITE)* was able to convince the teams he led that they were capable of winning. That, in a nutshell, is the definition of leadership.

The head coach of the Kansas City Chiefs, Marty Schottenheimer, had always admired Joe Montana from afar, so when the opportunity to sign the legendary quarterback as a free agent presented itself in 1993, Schottenheimer jumped.

Montana was thirty-seven years old—ancient by NFL standards—and he was coming off a serious elbow injury, but Schottenheimer looked past the battered body. He knew that Montana had the intangible gifts of a leader. In the season's sixth game, against the Chargers, Schottenheimer saw those gifts displayed.

"The guy has an unusual ability to forget about the play just concluded," Schottenheimer says. "And that, at least in one man's opinion, is the reason he has been able to do the things he has done.

"We saw the first evidence of Joe's history against San Diego. That drive to victory he threw 3 passes, 1 on first down, second, and third, that anybody here could have thrown. They were not very good passes. Yet, on fourth down, he made a throw moving to his left, to Willie Davis, that was the finest throw he has made this

season. Junior Seau's hand was there; the ball hit Willie between the '8' and the '4' on his jersey.

"To me, it was the proof that he doesn't worry about the plays that are gone. He only deals with the next one. It's characteristic of those who have that rare ability to bring a team back. Joe is able to deal with the circumstance as it relates solely to that individual situation."

So what is that intangible quality that allows Montana to lead men successfully on missions even they might not think possible? Even Montana acknowledges that he doesn't really know how to isolate the qualities of a good leader.

"People ask me about it, and I can't really put a finger on it," Montana says. "People talk about being afraid to be in certain situations. Listen, I don't like being in tough spots, but I'm not afraid to be there.

"I think that's how it is with this team [the Chiefs] and with the 49ers and at Notre Dame. You could get to the point where you're down and you could just say it's over, but not myself. No matter how you feel about it, if your teammates don't have confidence in you or you in them, nothing will get accomplished offensively."

Certainly, Montana is more than a cool, cerebral triggerman. Any NFL quarterback must have the prerequisites of athletic talent.

"He's a great athlete," says Bill Walsh, Montana's former coach with the 49ers. "Some people overlook that part of it. He has great body control, beautifully coordinated movement, and agility. Beyond that, he's courageous, instinctive, and resourceful."

All of this is confirmed by Randy Cross, who was Montana's center. "But there are just some people who have an unbelievable edge, and most of that edge is mental, not physical," according to Cross. "Joe has that same kind of edge. He has the ability to sharpen on what has to be done, and the ability to improvise. You can put a play up on the blackboard, but that isn't necessarily going to be the play he runs. He'll take it and improve it."

Perhaps former 49ers quarterback Guy Benjamin has the best spin on what makes Montana the quintessential leader. "Joe can't throw the ball hard and he's not a great runner," Benjamin says. "It's all inside. He has those intangibles. He has tremendous drive. He will not let another quarterback step on the field, and he'll play hurt. The great ones all have that drive. It's almost fear. His whole identity is being Joe Montana."

A single snapshot from Montana's marvelous scrapbook illustrates the workings of a charismatic leader. After suffering from a severe fever that forced him to lie down at halftime, Montana drove Notre Dame to 3 fourth-quarter touchdowns to beat Houston in the 1979 Cotton Bowl. The performance wasn't lost on Walsh, who drafted Montana in the third round.

"My feeling was that, if he could do it occasionally, we could coach him to do it regularly," Walsh says. "He had had some big games in college, so why not have a series of them with us?"

A SECOND-RATE SYSTEM

There is no satisfactory way to gauge true leadership outside the huddle or beyond the victory column. It is a quality that can't accurately be quantified. The next best thing (and it is a distant second) is the passer rating the NFL uses to rank quarterbacks.

It is based on the five statistics a quarterback generates: attempts, completions, yards, touchdowns, and interceptions. The formula is complicated, but generally speaking a passer is rewarded for efficiency. That means a high completion percentage and a low interception percentage will score well in the ratings.

As the purists point out, the problem with the passer rating is that it does not accurately represent the efforts of a gutsy quarterback trying to bring his team back from the brink of defeat. Although that quarterback is trying to save the game, he is penalized for trying to force a pass where it doesn't fit (often into the arms of a defender). Thus, until 1993, Denver's John Elway (who has made the eleventh hour his special purview) never compiled an impressive rating. Conversely, the more conservative approaches of Dave Krieg and Ken O'Brien produced

two of the best all-time career ratings ever (eleventh and seventeenth, respectively).

Sometimes, however, statistics don't lie. The three best career rankings of all time belong to Steve Young (96.8), Joe Montana (92.3), and Dan Marino (88.2), all three of whom should one day be in the Hall of Fame.

All were blessed to play in marvelous offensive systems that featured their unique abilities. All three put up heavy numbers and enjoyed remarkable touchdown-to-interception ratios. Montana, for example, had thrown 273 touchdowns—with only 139 interceptions—after the 1994 season.

The passer rating formula is also an inaccurate tool when used to compare quarterbacks from different eras because it rewards the pass-happy offenses of today. Eleven of the twenty top-rated passers played into the 1990s, including four of the top five; Otto Graham (86.6) is the only quarterback from a previous era to be represented. Only six Hall of Famers—Graham, Roger Staubach, Sonny Jurgensen, Len Dawson, Bart Starr, and Fran Tarkenton—are among the top twenty.

GETTING IT DONE

After his Minnesota Vikings went 1-4 against playoff teams in 1992, head coach Dennis Green traced the team's failure to its quarterbacks. In Green's estimation, Rich Gannon and Sean Salisbury did not exactly possess the stuff of champions. Green was fortunate because 1993 was the league's first year of unadulterated free agency. Quarterbacks with pedigrees were plentiful. And yet, he ultimately chose a thirty-four-year-old passer with a battered body and an apparent attitude: Jim McMahon.

One preseason publication went so far as to say, "Any team that counts on McMahon might as well count itself out."

McMahon did have a gruesome injury history, including broken bones, wrenched shoulders and knees, and a lacerated kidney. He had played in only 10 games in a season twice since leading the Chicago Bears to victory in Super Bowl XX in 1985. But Green had done his homework. McMahon had a phenomenal record against teams in the Vikings' NFC Central Division. And, wonder of wonders, McMahon's winning percentage was the second among active quarterbacks, behind Montana.

"There's nothing I can do to control injuries, and I really don't worry about it," McMahon said before the season. "I'm just going to play every game like it's my last. If I last, I last. If I don't...rehab again."

Oddly enough, McMahon lasted through the season and the Vikings finished with a 9-7 record and made the playoffs. And though Minnesota lost to the New York Giants, McMahon was valiant in defeat. This was the same McMahon who had played through pain in Chicago and who had guided the Philadelphia Eagles to an 8-3 record when Randall Cunningham was injured.

Philadelphia trainer Otho Davis likes to tell the story of McMahon's 1991 game in Cleveland.

McMahon's throwing elbow, nagged by tendinitis, reacted badly to a Friday injection of Novocaine, and the quarterback woke up at 6 A.M. with his elbow swollen to about the size of a baked potato.

"People who work regular office jobs, who don't use their bodies the way a pro athlete does, would've gotten up, taken a couple of aspirins, and gone back to bed," Davis says. "A lot of football players, too. They would've gotten up, taken a look at themselves and said, 'Ohhh man, so much for today.' Jimmy Mac got up, got on the phone and said, 'Let's get to work on it.' "

Six hours later, after constant massaging and another injection, McMahon walked on the field and produced the second-best passing day of his career. He threw 43 times for 341 yards and 3 touchdowns in a memorable 32-20 come-from-behind win.

"You wonder how he does it, unless you know him," Davis said. "The guy just is an amazing competitor, an amazing person. Pain and discomfort just are not concerns of his. They just aren't. Playing and winning are. I'll tell you one thing, they don't make many like Jimmy Mac anymore. Not today."

McMahon's heroic efforts are emblematic of leadership by example. Eagles quarterback coach Zeke Bratkowski had seen this sort of performance before. "Bart Starr, if you'd meet him, he's one of the most perfect gentleman you ever met in your life," Bratkowski says. "But put him on the football field, he'll cut your heart out and show it to you. And then after the game, he'll come over and shake your hand and say, 'Nice job.'

"Jimmy's like that, so intense with what he wants to do and has to do. His work ethic, his leadership is just unbelievable."

LEADERSHIP AS PRIVILEGE

Onetime Giants quarterback Phil Simms believes that leadership extends beyond the field, that it is particularly valuable in the locker room. But the esteem of a quarterback's peers doesn't just happen; such respect must first be won on the gridiron.

"Players feed off results and facts, things like that," Simms says. "If you want to be a leader, you've got to be a player—on the field. Once you're a player and you have that possibility of taking a team down the field, then you can exert yourself, use your influence off the field."

Green Bay quarterback Brett Favre is cut from the go-for-it McMahon/Simms mold. And unlike McMahon and Simms, who in their prime played for teams built around savage defenses, Favre finds himself in the enviable position of having a coach who understands offense. His head coach is Mike Holmgren, who was previously the offensive coordinator for the San Francisco 49ers when a guy named Montana was the quarterback.

Green Bay general manager Ron Wolf says Favre has some of the intangibles that were characteristic of Montana. "It's [Favre's] leadership ability," Wolf says.

"You can feel his presence on the field. He had everything else. By sitting and watching him play a game, you could feel that. By watching him in practice, you could feel that [leadership]...."

Certainly, Green Bay wide receiver Sterling Sharpe would agree. With Favre playing quarterback, Sharpe caught a record-setting 108 passes in 1992. Then in 1993, Sharpe broke his record with 112 catches. Favre will never have a top-rated passer rating (24 interceptions dragged his rating down to 72.2), but he, Sharpe, and Holmgren have the combined skills to insure that the future in Green Bay is bright.

Of course, there are subtler ways to lead a team to victory, too. Listen to Warren Central High School coach Jerry Staufer talk about former player Jeff George, now with the Atlanta Falcons. "He was never a rah-rah guy," Stauffer says. "He led simply by doing. He never, never raised his voice. I don't think that on more than one or two occasions in three years' time did he ever get mad at somebody for not doing what they were supposed to do.

"The only time he ever got mad at someone was for not trying. He doesn't expect anything out of anyone else that he doesn't give himself."

ABOVE: **Brett Favre of the Green Bay Packers has uncommon charisma in the huddle and an arm to go with it.**

OPPOSITE: **To Phil Simms, "leadership" is not idle locker room chatter; it is something proven in the crucible of battle. To illustrate: Simms authored the most efficient Super Bowl game in history, defeating the Denver Broncos in Super Bowl XXI.**

CHAPTER THREE

THE NEXT GENERATION

Since the Class of '83, when gunslingers named Elway, Marino, and Kelly arrived from the college ranks, the National Football League has been waiting patiently for the next generation of quarterbacks. As the 1980s met the 1990s, there were no saviors in sight. NFL personnel experts blamed the option schemes favored by many offensive college coaches. They blamed skateboards and video games—even soccer— for the dearth of quarterback talent.

Then, in 1993, the first two players taken in the draft were quarterbacks. The New England Patriots, the league's worst team in 1992, chose first overall and placed their future in the hands of Washington State's Drew Bledsoe. Seattle, picking second, took Notre Dame's Rick Mirer. This, in itself, was a piece of history; not since 1971—when Jim Plunkett, a future Super Bowl MVP, went to the Patriots and Archie Manning was scooped up by the New Orleans Saints—had quarterbacks gone first and second in the draft.

Immediately, Patriots head coach Bill Parcells and his Seahawks counterpart, Tom Flores, were inundated with the obvious question: would Bledsoe and Mirer— the long-awaited heirs apparent—start for their fledgling teams? After all, it had been an even two decades since two rookie quarterbacks had started for their teams (Joe Ferguson in Buffalo and Bert Jones in Baltimore).

"No," said Parcells, with emphasis. "No, I don't think so. I've never been a guy to throw anybody to the wolves. I can tell all the fans and all the people in the NFL, he'll play when he's ready."

Bledsoe entered training camp third on the Patriots' quarterback depth chart, behind Scott Secules and Scott Zolak. Mirer was up against Stan Gelbaugh and Dan McGwire, and had the discomforting knowledge that he was the third first-round quarterback to be drafted by the Seahawks in five years. Both players arrived late, after their agents had hammered out multimillion-dollar deals. Both young men got their clocks cleaned the first few days of practice.

"Although I had an advantage coming from a school where there was a lot of pressure, the time demands are pretty strenuous," Mirer said early on. "I don't have to worry about things like going to school, but football has become ten times more complicated.

"Nothing is really different. Everything is just a little better. The coverage by the defensive backs, for instance. You don't have guys who are just wide-open the way you would a lot of times in college.

"Here, we're stepping up to a new level with strength and speed and age and wisdom. They know what you are thinking and what you are trying to do to them. It makes it a little bit harder to get your job done."

Mirer, at six feet two inches and 216 pounds, differed from the six-foot-five-inch, 233-pound Bledsoe physically and in terms of styles of play. Coming from Notre Dame, Mirer had seen better competition and was more polished than Bledsoe going into the professional ranks. The scouts rated his courage, charisma, and leadership ahead of Bledsoe's. And while Mirer was more agile and a better risk scrambling out of the pocket,

In 1994, his second season as a professional, Drew Bledsoe, just twenty-two years old, became the youngest player ever named to the Pro Bowl. He also helped the New England Patriots into the playoffs and set a new league record for passing attempts, with 691.

Bledsoe possessed superior arm strength and marginally better accuracy.

Both players were installed as starters before the regular season.

"[Mirer] is the best we have," said Flores, a former quarterback, after McGwire suffered a broken bone in his throwing wrist. "People expect Rick to walk on water, but it's not fair to make a prediction. If he doesn't live up to it, then he's going to get criticized. Not by me, but by others."

Said Parcells of Bledsoe, "He's ready. Of course, the term 'ready' is a little ambiguous. He can be a heck of a lot more ready than he is. Hopefully, as the year goes on, he will become more ready."

Predictably, things did not go too well for either Bledsoe or Mirer. Remember, their teams were a combined 4-28 the year before. The two rookies met in the season's third game. Both teams were 0-2, and Mirer came away with the first victory. The Seahawks won a sloppy game 17-14 at Foxboro Stadium, but there were encouraging signs.

The first confrontation between Bledsoe and Mirer drew widespread interest around the country. After the game, the media pressed both coaches.

"Listen," Parcells said, smiling, "we're not going to find out what kind of quarterback this guy is going to be until after he's been sacked five times, he's thrown 4 interceptions, he's bleeding from the mouth, and his team has been beaten very badly, and he had a lot to do with it. And the reporters are up there asking him, 'Well, gee, Drew, it looked like you threw into coverage.' And all that.

"Can he get on the bus and go back and go to that practice field and say, 'Hey, I'm going to do better next week.' And if he can't do that, then he's not going to be a real good quarterback. And if he can, then eventually I think he will."

By season's end, with the final results in, it was clear Bledsoe and Mirer both had enormous futures—even though the early returns were not scintillating.

Bledsoe's passer rating of 65.0 was the league's third-worst figure, and Mirer's 67.0 wasn't much better. While Mirer completed 56.4 percent of his passes (compared to 49.9 for Bledsoe) and threw for more yards (2,833 to 2,494), Bledsoe threw 15 touchdown passes, balanced by 15 interceptions. Mirer had 12 scoring passes and 17 interceptions.

The big numbers, however, were 5 and 6. That's how many victories the Patriots and Seahawks collected in 1993, respectively, with Bledsoe and Mirer in the saddle. And the numbers are likely to improve for years to come.

"Hopefully, this sort of thing between Drew and I will go on for a long time," Mirer says. "You have Marino and Elway, who came in together. This is their eleventh year, and people are still talking about them. You know, I don't feel like competing against one guy forever. But we can build a pretty good friendship, and we have a lot of things in common."

Bledsoe was so convincing in the 1994 opener against Miami that Marino said, "Bledsoe played a great game. [He's] the next great quarterback in the league." Bledsoe went on to have a great season.

THROWN INTO THE PIT(S)

Like Bledsoe and Mirer, John Elway was thrown immediately into the fray. Like Bledsoe and Mirer, well....

"It was the absolute pits," Elway says. "I remember after the first couple of starts I had, I started talking to myself, 'Boy, what did I get myself into? They can have their money back, they can have everything. I don't like football anymore.' "

That's the universal reaction that highly touted rookie quarterbacks share when they join the battle in the NFL. Name any respected quarterback—Elway or Marino, Staubach or Bradshaw—and chances are they all struggled initially with the complex game plans, the larger, faster defenses, and the pressure of the position.

After an impressive preseason performance by John Elway in 1983, then–Denver coach Dan Reeves con-

Seattle's Rick Mirer set a rookie record for pass attempts in 1993, with 486. In 1994, he threw a credible 11 touchdowns, balanced by only 7 interceptions.

vinced himself that the young quarterback was ready for the NFL. Elway started the first five games of the 1983 regular season. He did not start the next five—Reeves benched Elway in favor of backup Steve DeBerg.

"Physically, John was ready to play," Reeves says. "Mentally, it was like a different language."

When DeBerg was injured in the tenth game, against Seattle, Elway came on in relief. He started 4 more games and finished his rookie season with 7 touchdowns, 14 interceptions, and a passer rating under 55.0.

"You look back, thrown to the wolves and those type of things, where everything was flying over my head and I didn't know what was going on. But that helped me so much, in growing up in a hurry and maturing, and getting me to the position that I wanted to be in."

Since the merger between the American Football League and the National Football League in 1970, only twelve rookie quarterbacks have opened the season as starters. Elway, Bledsoe, and Mirer actually came away relatively unscathed. Consider the sorry debut season of Terry Bradshaw. The Pittsburgh Steelers made him the first pick in the entire 1970 draft, but the Louisiana Tech star stumbled badly in his first season: the Steelers finished 5-9, and Bradshaw threw 6 touchdown passes and 24 interceptions. Nineteen years later, he was in the Pro Football Hall of Fame.

Archie Manning's first season in New Orleans was a disaster—6 touchdown passes and 9 interceptions—but he later found his equilibrium. Bert Jones (4 touchdowns, 12 interceptions), Doug Williams (7 touchdowns, 8 interceptions), Jeff George (16 touchdowns, 13 interceptions), and Joe Ferguson (4 touchdowns, 10 interceptions) all enjoyed marvelous college careers only to struggle as rookies.

And then there is Troy Aikman. The Dallas Cowboys made him the first overall choice in the 1989 draft; the rest of the league then spent his rookie season wondering why. Coach Jimmy Johnson committed to Aikman in training camp, and the UCLA athlete wound up with 9 touchdown passes and 18 interceptions.

"Aikman was thrown into it and he was beat around," says former Cowboys quarterback Roger Staubach. "The team was 1-15. But it just depends on your mental attitude. I mean, either you learn from it or you can get depressed from it and it actually affects the rest of your life.

"Maybe Jeff George is somebody who was affected by it, by not handling it. Aikman fought through it and now he's a world champion; it's mostly a mental thing. Any quarterback going in early is going to be at a disadvantage, but you must learn from it, get better quicker.

"You've got to realize, 'Hey, I'm going to make some mistakes, but I'm improving.' A quarterback with a lot of self-confidence and self-esteem is going to be able to go in there and deal with it."

ANOTHER PRIZED PAIR

Just when Bledsoe and Mirer were working themselves back into shape for their sophomore seasons, another dazzling pair of quarterbacks joined the NFL fraternity. The Washington Redskins—who had already parted ways with Super Bowl XXVI MVP Mark Rypien—drafted Tennessee quarterback Heath Shuler third overall. The man behind the decision was rookie head coach Norv Turner, who had previously been Aikman's mentor as the Dallas offensive coordinator. Shuler was six feet two inches and 221 pounds, and was coming off a season in which he threw a school-record 25 touchdown passes. He was also runner-up to Florida State quarterback Charlie Ward (who never made it to the NFL) in the Heisman Trophy balloting.

After the Patriots selected University of Southern California defensive end Willie McGinest fourth overall and the Colts took Nebraska linebacker Trev Alberts fifth, the Tampa Bay Buccaneers jumped on Fresno State quarterback Trent Dilfer as the sixth overall choice. Dilfer, at six feet three inches and 228 pounds, had led the nation's collegiate players in passing, throwing 271 passes without an interception.

Dilfer, because of his size and strength, was compared by many league scouts to Bledsoe, while the smaller Shuler was likened to Mirer in terms of mobility and attitude. In a way, there was less pressure on Shuler and Dilfer, for Bledsoe and Mirer had already proven rookie quarterbacks could survive the NFL.

"We've allowed them to see they can step in and do it," Bledsoe says. "At the same time, historically, you don't see too many quarterbacks step right in and light it up. We were reasonably successful. If they come in and work hard, they can expect the same level of success."

After a year of comparisons, Shuler and Dilfer know what is possible.

"They set the standards for the rest of the quarterbacks, as far as young guys coming in," Shuler says. "Regardless of experience, you can play."

OPPOSITE: **Heath Shuler looked impressive in the Washington Redskins' 1994 minicamp. He later finished his rookie season as the league's lowest-ranked quarterback, but there were signs he would be effective in 1995.**

LEFT: **NFL Commissioner Paul Tagliabue smiled when the Tampa Bay Buccaneers made Trent Dilfer (RIGHT) their first-round draft choice in the 1994 draft. As a rookie, Dilfer played behind Craig Erickson and attempted only 82 passes.**

CHAPTER FOUR

SUPER BOWL MOMENTS

In the week leading up to Super Bowl XXII, Redskins quarterback Doug Williams was scrutinized from every possible angle, but the main focus of the media frenzy was that Doug Williams would make history on January 31, 1988, as the first black quarterback to start in football's ultimate game.

Williams, a bastion of calm, handled all the intense pressure well. He stood patiently as reporters asked the same questions over and over again. He talked endlessly about the competitive attitude that he had developed growing up in an eight-child, five-boy family in Zachary, Louisiana—an approach to sports that was crystalized at Chaneyville High School, which was integrated during his senior year. He talked about the frustration of careers that never came together at Grambling University, in the United States Football League, and with the Tampa Bay Buccaneers of the National Football League.

"How long have you been a black quarterback?" asked one reporter.

Williams, who was as astonished at the stupidity of the question as the other reporters surrounding him on Media Day (the Tuesday before the Super Bowl), had the good grace to smile before asking if the question might be rephrased. He took it all in stride. After all, this was just show business. Williams knew the real world could be a grim place; his wife of eleven months, Janice

Goss Williams, had died suddenly in 1983. Everything considered, there was an undeniable pressure on him.

"I didn't do this for Black America," Williams said. "I did it for the Redskins."

Washington had gone 11-4 during the regular season, before erasing Chicago and Minnesota in the playoffs leading to the Super Bowl meeting with the Denver Broncos. But the Broncos, who had been trashed the year before by the New York Giants 39-20 in Super Bowl XXI, were driven by thoughts of revenge. They were favored to win by a field goal.

When the Redskins found themselves in a 10-0 first-quarter hole, it appeared that the oddsmakers had handicapped the game correctly. What they hadn't counted on was the strength of will of Doug Williams. The Redskins and Williams made history that day at Jack Murphy Stadium. Washington became the first team in NFL postseason history to score 5 touchdowns in a single quarter. Those 5 touchdowns—35 points—were scored in 5 consecutive second-quarter possessions. It took Washington fifteen minutes of game time to do it. The previous record was 21 points, accomplished by the Chicago Bears in Super Bowl XX and the San Francisco 49ers in Super Bowl XIX.

"I kept looking at the little '35' in the second-quarter box on the scoreboard," said tight end Don Warren. "Wow. It was almost unreal. You don't score 35 points

In the space of just fifteen minutes during Super Bowl XXII, Doug Williams of the Washington Redskins threw an astonishing 5 touchdown passes.

ABOVE, LEFT TO RIGHT: **Greatness under pressure is illustrated by the following: Joe Montana in Super Bowl XXIV, Terry Bradshaw in Super Bowl XIV, and Bart Starr in Super Bowl II.**

OPPOSITE: **Giants quarterback Phil Simms completed 22 of 25 passes against the Denver Broncos in Super Bowl XXI, for a record 88 percent.**

in a quarter, especially against the Denver Broncos, especially in the Super Bowl.''

Here is the dazzling second-quarter wreckage wrought by Williams, who played the game wearing a cumbersome brace on his sprained left knee and recovering from emergency root-canal surgery the day before: 357 yards in 18 plays—in a total possession time of five minutes and forty-seven seconds. There were 80- and 50-yard scoring passes to wide receiver Ricky Sanders, a 27-yard pass to wideout Gary Clark, and a modest 8-yard touchdown pass to tight end Clint Didier. Somewhere in the middle of all that, rookie running back Timmy Smith slashed through a hole at left tackle and ran 58 yards for another score.

"I can't put my finger on it," Williams said. "The receivers just ran great routes and I just put the ball in their hands."

As the two coaches walked off the field at the end of the game, Washington's Joe Gibbs sought out his close friend Dan Reeves. "I'm sorry, Dan," Gibbs said. "This was the best game we played all season long—and it happened to be the Super Bowl."

And Williams, who completed 18 of 29 passes for 340 yards, had the game of his life in the crucible of the Super Bowl.

Naturally, Williams was the runaway choice for the game's MVP award—after all, his performance had changed the momentum in Super Bowl XXII. In fact, through Super Bowl XXVIII, quarterbacks had won fifteen of the twenty-eight MVP awards. San Francisco's Joe Montana took home three new cars in four appearances—and some critics argued that he should have been 4-for-4. Terry Bradshaw of the Pittsburgh Steelers won back-to-back MVPs in Super Bowls XIII and XIV.

The Green Bay Packers' Bart Starr won the game's first two MVP awards in 1967 and 1968.

THE DAY OF THE UNDERDOG

While Montana, Bradshaw, and Starr were predictable heroes for powerful teams that transcended their era, Williams was a complete long shot. So, too, was Phil Simms the year before Washington's postseason victory, in Super Bowl XXI. While most people were focusing on the Golden Boy, Denver's John Elway, Simms merely went about his business.

"When you think of the Denver Broncos, you think of John Elway," Simms said. "When you think of the Giants, you don't think of me.

"I'm not the prettiest thing, but I'm productive. You look at me and John Elway the last three years, I've been more productive than he has, but nobody cares."

Indeed, Simms threw for more yards than Elway each season in 1984 and 1985 (and in 1986, Elway beat him by just 52 yards). Simms also threw as many or more touchdowns in all three seasons.

"I guess they figure Denver won't win if Elway doesn't play well and that it doesn't matter what I do," Simms said.

On January 25, 1987, Phil Simms' performance mattered very much to the New York Giants. Quite simply, it was the difference between winning and losing.

Even at halftime, with his team trailing, Simms told teammates it would be all right, that he would carry the Giants. "I could just feel it," Simms said. "I could feel it all week that I was going to have a good game. I don't know if I was trying to psyche myself up for the game or what, but I told a few players, I just said, 'Hey, I've got it working today.'"

Said left tackle Brad Benson, one of Simms' closest friends, "He was walking around saying, 'Hey, I know I can get them.' He's been through a lot of injuries, a lot of criticism. People always said he could never win the big game. Well, they don't get any bigger than this."

Simms completed 22 of 25 passes for 268 yards. His completion percentage of 88.0 was the highest in Super Bowl history. It was also the highest mark ever recorded in all 213 previous postseason NFL games. Simms, with a decidedly mediocre corps of receivers, threw 3 touchdown passes. He did not throw any interceptions. He completed 10 of 10 passes in the second half, when the Giants erased a 10-9 deficit and buried the Broncos, 39-20.

"I thought Phil Simms was unbelievable," said Giants coach Bill Parcells. "That's as good a game as has ever been played by a quarterback."

"I don't think there was one ball today where I said, 'Geez, I wish I could have that one back,'" said Simms, who had thrown 8 touchdowns and no interceptions in 3 playoff games that year. "It's a good feeling as a quarterback to know, 'Well, I'll probably complete it. I don't know who to. But I'll get it to somebody.'"

It was, as Giants left guard Bill Ard pointed out, a Waltonian performance. "He pulled a Walton today," Ard said, referring to the 1973 NCAA basketball final in which UCLA center Bill Walton made 21 of 22 shots against Memphis State.

"He had a career day," Ard said. "He had a career we've always known he would have."

EXTRAORDINARY JOE

Discussions about quarterbacking always seem to come back to Joe Montana, the lean gunslinger who won four Super Bowls for the San Francisco 49ers. Going into the 1994 season, he was the highest-rated quarterback in football history, and he always seemed to save his best games for those times when the stakes were highest.

When he reached his first Super Bowl, the one in Detroit with the Roman numerals XVI, Montana was twenty-five years old. He had already slain the Dallas Cowboys with "The Catch," a nifty 7-yard touchdown pass to a leaping Dwight Clark. Montana was, by all accounts, nervous and edgy all week long leading up to San Francisco's meeting with the Cincinnati Bengals.

But on the 49ers' first drive, Montana threw on 5 of the first 6 plays and capped a 68-yard drive by scoring on a quarterback sneak. That was the end of any Super Bowl jitters. In the second quarter, Montana led the 49ers on a 92-yard touchdown drive. Two more drives netted 2 more field goals and secured a rock-solid 20-0 lead for San Francisco.

"It was the machinelike precision of the offense that Joe directed," says Bill Walsh, the former 49ers' coach. "It was diversity and execution, and Joe was the primer who could make the delicate play when he had to. Our drives in the first half of that Super Bowl were comparable to that drive against Dallas. Joe was letter-perfect."

The 49ers won 26-21, and Montana, who had completed 14 of 22 passes for 157 yards and no interceptions, collected his first MVP award.

San Francisco returned to the Super Bowl three years later, but Montana was virtually ignored. This was because Miami quarterback Dan Marino had set an NFL record with 48 touchdown passes over the 1984 regular season. But it was Montana who ultimately won the game, with guile more than anything.

Montana had never been much of a runner, but on that day on the Stanford University playing field he scrambled five times for 59 yards, and his runs set up 2 of the 49ers' first 3 touchdowns. San Francisco won 38-16, and Montana set records for passing yards (331) and total offense (537 yards). In two Super Bowls, Montana had won two MVP awards.

Following Super Bowl XXIII, most people who followed football would have argued that Montana should have been 3-for-3. The 49ers trailed the Cincinnati Bengals 16-13 with just three minutes and ten seconds left in the game at Joe Robbie Stadium in Miami. Starting at his own 8 yard line, Montana rallied San Francisco in heroic fashion.

"At times like that," Montana says, "you get into a certain mode on the field and everything else is blocked out, like how much time is left. It's really secondary at that point. You're really trying to live each play for that

After the San Francisco 49ers had vanquished the Denver Broncos in Super Bowl XXIV, Joe Montana collected his third Most Valuable Player award in four Super Bowls.

play and not looking forward to the next play, because if you don't keep moving the ball forward you won't have anything. I guess you can call it living for the moment."

Nevertheless, Montana began to hyperventilate at one point early in the drive.

"It was crazy," Montana says. "It had never happened to me before. I guess it was the excitement, maybe a little bit of the heat. At that point you couldn't hear, so I was yelling plays at the top of my voice. Maybe it was because I used all of my oxygen—I had to call everything about eight times—and it took everything I had. I was just standing there and I went blank. I thought I was going to completely pass out. When I walked up to the center, I thought for sure I was going to have to call a time-out. Then, my head seemed to clear, but as I took the snap that dizzy feeling came back."

The result was an incomplete pass to wide receiver Jerry Rice. But a few plays later, Montana hit Rice with a crucial 27-yard pass that moved the ball to the Cincinnati 18 yard line. With thirty-four seconds left on the clock, Montana threw a 10-yard pass to wide receiver John Taylor for the winning touchdown.

Rice, who caught 11 of Montana's passes for a Super Bowl record of 215 yards, was named the MVP. But many believed that Montana's nearly unconscious 23-for-36, 357 yards, and 2 touchdowns merited the award.

The next year, in Super Bowl XXIV, Montana made history with his third MVP award. He completed 22 of 29 passes for 297 yards and 5 touchdowns without an interception. In New Orleans, the 49ers crushed the hapless Denver Broncos 55-10, the game's biggest rout.

It was San Francisco's fourth Super Bowl victory in as many tries, equaling the record set by Pittsburgh. In four Super Bowls, Montana's numbers are impeccable: 83 completions, 122 attempts, 1,142 yards, 11 touchdowns, no interceptions. His Super Bowl rating of 127.8 is off the charts.

"What can you say about a guy who saves his best games for the Super Bowl?" Walsh asks. "I guess you could call him a Hall of Famer."

CHAPTER FIVE

THE GREATEST QUARTERBACKS OF ALL TIME

Whether the game of football is played on a patch of playground dirt, a high school field, or a sold-out arena, the quarterback is always the focus of attention. He touches the ball on every offensive play and is charged with delivering that ball to a teammate.

As glamorous and exciting as it looks, this clearly is no day at the beach. Swift, powerful linebackers, 300-pound defensive linemen, and blitzing safeties would all like to separate the quarterback from the ball, not to mention his senses.

It takes a man of a particular mindset to play the position well. He must possess both the fire necessary to inspire his team and the cool to remain detached and analytical. He must have the strength to throw the ball 40 yards downfield and the subtlety to feather a short screen pass over outstretched hands. He must have the split-second intuition and imagination necessary to discard one option and go with another.

The quarterbacks gathered here are the best football has ever known. They are all profiled, from the precise passing of the Dallas Cowboys' Troy Aikman to the raw charisma of Joe Namath of the New York Jets to the intelligence of the Baltimore Colts' Johnny Unitas. Matching gems Joe Montana and Steve Young, two of history's greatest, both of whom happen to have played for the San Francisco 49ers at the same time, are included. Here also is the Miami Dolphin's Dan Marino, who is on the threshold of owning the league's most coveted records. Bart Starr of the Green Bay Packers, a winner by any definition in any era, is also featured.

These men are individuals, each of whom has a different approach to the game, but they are united by their greatness on the gridiron.

ABOVE: Dan Marino is a fierce competitor with an arsenal of offensive weapons. He, too, is one of the greatest quarterbacks ever to play the game.

OPPOSITE: San Francisco has been blessed with two of the greatest quarterbacks of all time. Steve Young is the latest of the two.

TROY AIKMAN

In 1989 the Dallas Cowboys borrowed a page from the Pittsburgh Steelers' history book. Head coach Jimmy Johnson, a shrewd judge of talent, made UCLA quarterback Troy Aikman the first overall pick in the draft. Johnson envisioned Aikman as the cornerstone of a dynasty—just as Chuck Noll had seen Louisiana Tech quarterback Terry Bradshaw as the Steelers' future in 1970.

Bradshaw and Noll wound up with four Super Bowl rings, but the only thing the Dallas Cowboys found in Aikman's rookie season was heartache. But lost in that disturbing final record of 1-15 were the seeds of Johnson's long-term plan. There were handfuls of trades; free agents were rushed in and out of the lineup; and only a 13-3 victory at Washington—with Aikman on the sidelines—spared the Cowboys the humiliation of going 0-for-16.

The one constant in personnel was the six-foot-four-inch, 216-pound Aikman, who gradually grew into the job. He finished his rookie season with a modest 1,749 yards, 9 touchdowns, and 18 interceptions; the best quarterbacks generally enjoy a 2:1 ratio of touchdowns to interceptions.

The Cowboys improved dramatically in 1990, winning 7 and losing 9 games. Dallas might have made the playoff if Aikman hadn't missed the last 2 games due to injury. The gap between Aikman's critical numbers—touchdowns (11) and interceptions (18)—narrowed. In 1991 both team and individual numbers improved. The Cowboys were an 11-5 play-off team; Aikman threw 11 touchdowns and only 10 interceptions. His passer rating was the league's sixth-best, ahead of such leading lights as Dan Marino and Warren Moon.

In 1992 the steady, incremental progress blossomed into greatness. Aikman (23 touchdowns, 14 interceptions) was the league's third-best passer, and the Cowboys were 13-3 in the regular season. In the play-offs, Dallas and its quarterback found a new gear.

Philadelphia was dispatched 34-10, San Francisco fell 30-20, and in Super Bowl XXVII Buffalo was destroyed 52-17. Aikman, who completed 22 of 30 passes for 273 yards, 4 touchdowns, and no interceptions, was the Most Valuable Player. In 3 postseason games, Aikman threw 8 touchdowns and no interceptions. His passer rating for the playoffs (a scalding 116.7) broke Bart Starr's record of 104.8. Aikman, too, was the youngest quarterback to win the MVP since Joe Montana had won the award in Super Bowl XVI in 1982.

"I still don't fully understand the scope of what we've done," Aikman said after Super Bowl XXVII. "But slowly I'm beginning to realize that I now have a place in history with some other quarterbacks. The last two seasons, even though I'd had success, I don't think people perceived me as a top-notch quarterback. It took the Super Bowl for me to break out of that image.

"I know a tremendous weight has been taken off my shoulders, because where I was drafted, this is what's expected. You're expected to win a Super Bowl. That's what it's all about. That's not going to make me complacent, but at least I've done that, and now I can move forward."

And that's exactly what happened. Aikman's 1993 season was another personal best, his fifth straight year in an upward spiral. His passer rating of 99.0 was surpassed only by San Francisco's Steve Young, and the Cowboys rolled to their second straight Super Bowl victory, another blowout of Buffalo.

Only four quarterbacks have taken their team to consecutive Super Bowl titles: Bart Starr (1967 and 1968), Terry Bradshaw (1975 and 1976 and again in 1979 and 1980), Joe Montana (1989 and 1990), and Troy Aikman (1993 and 1994). The first two are in the Hall of Fame. The other two will one day join them.

OPPOSITE: **Dallas quarterback Troy Aikman weathered an abysmal 1-15 rookie season before blossoming into one of the league's most efficient passers. In this game early in the 1992 season, the Cowboys dispatched the Raiders 28-13.**

S A M M Y   B A U G H

There was a time when passes did not fill the air in National Football League games. Rather, football was a rather grim, grinding, ground-oriented affair. Sammy "Slinging Sammy" Baugh changed all that. He arrived in Washington as the first overall pick of the 1937 draft, and when the accomplished quarterback retired sixteen seasons later, the league was more wide-open and fan-friendly than it had ever been before.

Baugh might have been the best athlete ever to play the position. He attended Texas Christian University on a baseball scholarship and had actually signed with the St. Louis Cardinals baseball team when Redskins owner George Preston Marshall lured him to the NFL with a then-dazzling five-thousand-dollar contract. Marshall needed Baugh's charisma to help football take hold in the nation's capital.

Baugh was a lean six-foot-two-inch, 180-pound single-wing tailback whose versatility left opposing defenses guessing—and grasping at air. When Baugh received the snap from center, he had four options: pass the ball to a teammate, pitch the ball to a runner behind him, run it himself, or quick-kick the ball.

And although Baugh drew skepticism from his new Redskins coach, Ray Flaherty, he soon proved that passing was the wave of the future. In the College All-Star Game (during which the ranking national team played a team of college stars), Baugh's touchdown pass to Gaynell Tinsley provided the only points in a shocking 6-0 victory over the Green Bay Packers, the reigning league champions. In his debut, against the New York Giants, Baugh completed 11 of 16 passes in a 13-3 win. In the NFL championship, Baugh threw 3 long touchdown passes and totaled 335 yards in the air. A 35-yard toss to Ed Justice won the game over Chicago 28-21.

In eight seasons under Flaherty, Baugh was a very successful single-wing tailback. But in 1944, rookie coach Dudley DeGroot decided to use the new T-formation that was revolutionizing the game. Baugh was now positioned as a conventional quarterback, but his statistics were extraordinary.

In fact, the NFL record book is littered with the wreckage Baugh wrought. No man before or since Baugh ever led the league in passing six different times. Baugh, who did it over a remarkable stretch of thirteen seasons, is ahead of Len Dawson, Roger Staubach, and Ken Anderson, each of whom won four passing titles. Baugh also holds the record for leading the league the most times in completions (he is tied with Marino at 5) and attempts (he, Marino, Johnny Unitas, and George Blanda are tied at 4). And Baugh fashioned the league's best completion percentage in a season seven times, second only to Dawson's total of eight.

In 1945, in a season that was characterized by the changes Baugh had brought to the game, the quarterback completed 128 of 182 passes—good for a completion percentage of 70.33. Thirty-seven years later, when the NFL was entrenched as a pass-fancy league, Anderson inched past Baugh's record with a completion percentage of 70.55.

In the final analysis, Baugh's unrivaled versatility was his most breathtaking quality. Consider his 1943 season: Baugh led the league in passing, completing 133 of 239 passes for 1,754 yards, 23 touchdowns, and 19 interceptions; as a Washington defensive back—the good players played both offense and defense in that time—Baugh led the league with 11 interceptions; and he was the Redskins' punter—in fact, Baugh's lifetime average punt distance of 45.1 yards is the highest on record.

OPPOSITE: **Not only was Sammy Baugh a stellar quarterback; he was officially the greatest punter in the history of the game. Here, he kicks one over the outstretched hands of Brooklyn Dodgers opponents at Ebbets Field in 1940.**

TERRY BRADSHAW

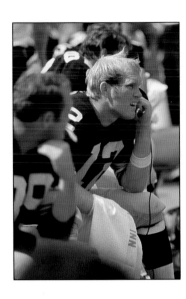

You will find the name Terry Bradshaw mentioned only once in the National Football League's list of official regular-season passing records. Way down, past the noteworthy areas of attempts, completions, yards, and touchdowns, he is mentioned under the category of average gain. In 1977 and 1978 Bradshaw led the NFL with the highest average gain. Sid Luckman of the Chicago Bears led all passers five times in this little-known category. Green Bay's Bart Starr did it three times. Bradshaw's two titles ties him with five others.

A team's average gain on pass plays is a product of the pressure the players exert on an opposing defense, and in the late 1970s the Pittsburgh Steelers stretched teams to the breaking point. Bradshaw is better remembered, of course, for leading the Steelers to a then-unprecedented four Super Bowl titles between the 1974 and 1979 seasons. In 2 of those games, Bradshaw was voted the Most Valuable Player, which is why you will find him today in Pro Football's Hall of Fame.

Bradshaw, a classic six-foot-three-inch, 210-pound bundle of muscle and grit, came to the Steelers from Louisiana Tech as the first pick of the 1970 draft. Pittsburgh won a coin flip with the Chicago Bears for the right to draft Bradshaw. But for four seasons, he was considered a disappointment; he managed to complete only 38.1 percent of his passes and threw a league-high 24 interceptions.

"My rookie season was a disaster," remembers Bradshaw, who is now an NFL analyst for the Fox network. "I was totally unprepared for pro ball. I had no schooling on reading defenses. I had never studied game film the way a quarterback should. I was an outsider who didn't mingle well. The other players looked on me as a Bible-toting Li'l Abner."

Two seasons later, Bradshaw guided the Steelers to the playoffs. By the 1974 season, Bradshaw had found himself. He was given complete control of the offense for the first time and he blossomed. The

RIGHT: **Terry Bradshaw, the first overall selection in the 1970 NFL draft, led the league in interceptions as a rookie before becoming one of the league's great passers. Here, Bradshaw prepares to fire one against the Oilers.**

Steelers were right in step. Pittsburgh was victorious in Super Bowl IX, 16-6 over the Minnesota Vikings. The next season, the Steelers defeated Dallas 21-17 in football's ultimate game, but Bradshaw's contributions were overlooked on both occasions. Steelers running back Franco Harris was the MVP in Super Bowl IX, and wide receiver Lynn Swann was the MVP in Super Bowl X. It was Bradshaw's sensational 64-yard touchdown pass to Swann that beat the Cowboys; Bradshaw never saw it because he had been knocked unconscious on the release.

Slowly, credit was given to Bradshaw, and he emerged as the biggest star on a team of future Hall of

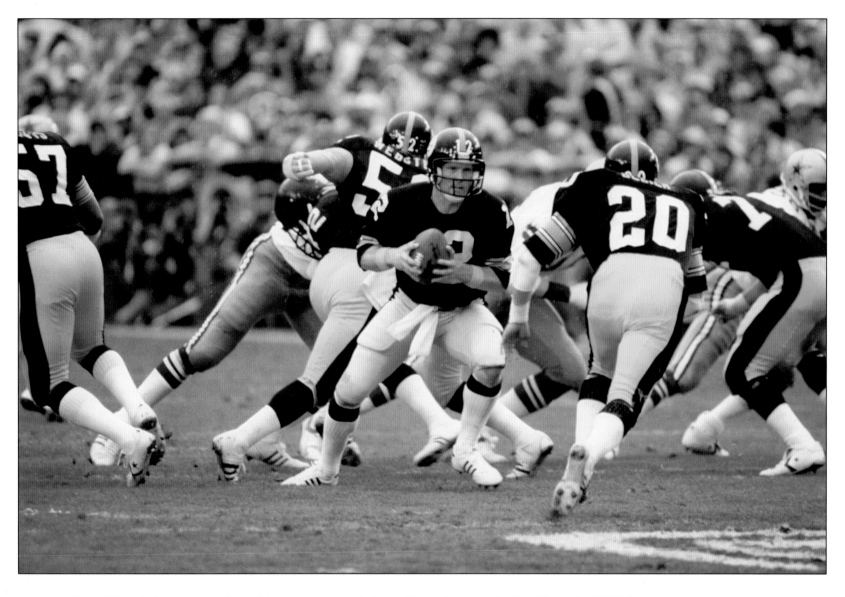

Famers. In 1978, eight seasons into his career, Bradshaw was voted by his peers to the Pro Bowl for the first time. That same season, in a scintillating 35-31 victory over Dallas in Super Bowl XIII, Bradshaw threw for 318 yards and 4 touchdowns, 2 to receiver John Stallworth. Finally, Bradshaw was rewarded by being named Most Valuable Player.

The following year, Bradshaw was elected to his second Pro Bowl. In Super Bowl XIV, he threw for 308 yards against the Los Angeles Rams. Swann caught a 47-yard touchdown pass and Stallworth reeled in a 73-yarder to make Bradshaw the MVP for the second time in a row and give the Steelers an unprecedented fourth Super Bowl title.

Bradshaw may not be a featured performer in the regular-season record book, but he owns the postseason edition. Bradshaw has the best average gain per pass, at 11.1, and is second to Joe Montana in yards and touchdowns. In 1989 Bradshaw had the last laugh on those who doubted his ability. Along with Steelers teammate Mel Blount, a peerless cornerback, Bradshaw was enshrined in Canton, Ohio.

Bradshaw played in four Super Bowls and was named the Most Valuable Player in two of them (including this one against the Cowboys, Super Bowl XIII).

JOHN ELWAY

His physical gifts—Elway can rifle the ball 50 yards down the field while running to his left—are only part of the package; Elway's intrinsic leadership skills routinely carry the Broncos to victories that seem out of reach. Through 1993, Elway had engineered a staggering 32 game-saving drives in the fourth quarter. The Broncos won 31 of those games and tied in the other.

And while Elway is one of the most decorated quarterbacks in football history and a certain pick for the Pro Football Hall of Fame, two things had eluded him through his first ten seasons. Two weeks after "The Drive," Denver lost Super Bowl XXI to the Giants. Ultimately, there would be 3 Super Bowl losses in a span of four seasons. Those in the league understood the overachieving Broncos would never have reached the league's marquee game without Elway, but some fans around the country questioned his heart.

Because of head coach Dan Reeves' conservative offense, Elway never had the chance to stand toe-to-toe with fellow members of the lauded Class of '83, such as Miami's Dan Marino and Buffalo's Jim Kelly. Even without a showcase offensive scheme, Elway managed to produce prolific numbers; heading into the 1994 season, Elway's nine years with 3,000 passing yards or more per season rank second in history to Marino's ten.

After the 1992 season, however, Reeves was fired and Elway was given the system he felt he deserved. "I've always been a bit jealous of Joe Montana," Elway admitted before the season. Elway responded with career bests in yards (4,030), touchdowns (25), and interceptions (10). His passer rating was 92.8, another best, and there was a delicious irony: Elway had the AFC's best rating and Montana (87.4) had the second-best.

The architect of the offense was one Jim Fassel, the man who recruited Elway at Stanford University and built a legendary offense around him. When Bill Walsh left Stanford for the San Francisco 49ers,

For more than a decade now, the enduring image of John Albert Elway is of the six-foot-three-inch, 215-pound athlete willing his Denver Broncos down the field as time winds down in the 1986 AFC Championship Game against Cleveland. Elway moved the Broncos 98 yards in 15 plays and hit wide receiver Mark Jackson with a 5-yard touchdown pass that sent the game into overtime. Denver prevailed 23-20, and "The Drive" became a part of NFL history.

THE GREATEST QUARTERBACKS OF ALL TIME

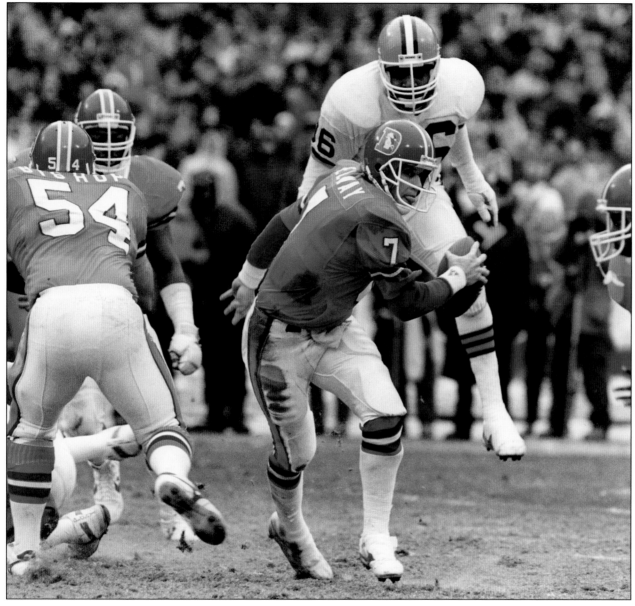

Accomplished Denver quarterback John Elway, here escaping airborne Cleveland defender Reggie Camp to keep "The Drive" alive, is still looking to win his first Super Bowl.

Fassell incorporated many of his offensive plays. Elway set five National Collegiate Athletic Association records at Stanford, including completions (774), attempts (1,243), and the lowest career interception percentage (3.13).

That Elway and the Denver Broncos found each other in 1983 was something of an upset. Elway, one of the best athletes ever to play quarterback, played for the New York Yankees single-A farm team in the summer of 1982. As a senior at Stanford, he hit .349 with 9 home runs and 50 RBIs in 49 games.

When the Baltimore Colts drafted him first overall in the 1983 draft, Elway threatened to play baseball for a living, but a trade to Denver changed his mind. And though Marino is destined to wind up first in the NFL record books, there are many who believe that if Elway had wound up in Miami, Elway's records would be unassailable.

DAN FOUTS

While San Diego rookie Dan Fouts was wrestling with complex offensive terminology and the swift, strong NFL defenses, a legendary player was starting at quarterback for the Chargers. His name was Johnny Unitas, and in the 1973 season's third game he became football's first 40,000-yard passer. Two weeks later, Fouts was the starter for the Chargers.

In 1986, when Fouts was on the verge of passing Unitas' historic total, he was humble: "He was my idol. I don't want to diminish anything he's ever done."

Today, they are both in the Pro Football Hall of Fame. Heading into the 1995 season, Fouts is third to Fran Tarkenton and Dan Marino in yardage (43,040), attempts (5,604), and completions (3,297).

Fouts was the spearhead of one of the league's great offenses from 1978 to 1985. In 1979, 1980, and 1981 Fouts passed for more than 4,000 yards each year. His total of 4,802 is the second-highest on record, after Dan Marino's 5,084 (accomplished in 1984). No one produced more 300-yard games than Fouts, who reached the magic number an amazing 51 times.

Fouts grew up in San Francisco, the son of Bob Fouts, a sportscaster who broadcasted 49ers games for many years. Fortunately for Fouts, he would later—through his father's connections—cross paths with two future 49ers coaches. George Seifert, then an assistant at the University of Oregon, was the first. "We've got a pro-type offense," Seifert told the high school senior, "and you can do the job for us."

Fouts attended Oregon and in three seasons passed for school records (at the time) of 5,995 yards and 37 touchdowns. San Diego coach Harland Svare chose Fouts in the draft over Louisiana State University's Bert Jones and Virginia Tech's Don Strock. Unitas was signed before the draft, mainly to serve as Fouts' mentor.

Unitas, by then thirty-nine years old, was injured in the fourth game of the season, and Fouts entered with the Chargers trailing the Pittsburgh Steelers 38-0. He finished with 174 yards and 1 touchdown; San Diego lost 38-21. Fouts developed quickly as a top-flight passer, but the Chargers were a combined 9-32-1 his first three seasons.

Things changed in 1976, when Bill Walsh arrived as the team's offensive coordinator. The record that season was 6-8, the team's best since 1971, and Fouts set personal bests in yardage (2,535) and touchdowns (14). Don Coryell joined the team as head coach in 1978 and the Chargers responded with a 9-7 record; the Chargers also led the league in passing, as they would for seven of the next eight seasons.

"Bill Walsh really got me in position to be an effective quarterback," says Fouts, today an NFL television analyst. "But when Coryell came, it was bombs away. It was a dream come true for any quarterback to play for him."

And so, the totals climbed. Fouts was not blessed with a powerful throwing arm, but his intelligence, quick drops, and defensive reads allowed him to throw exquisite timing patterns. With Fouts firing to an all-star cast of receivers—Charlie Joiner, Wes Chandler, John Jefferson, and tight end Kellen Winslow—the Chargers were virtually unstoppable.

In Fouts' most memorable game, the San Diego Chargers won a 41-38 overtime game against the Miami Dolphins in the first round of the 1981 playoffs. Fouts completed 33 of 53 passes for 433 yards. San Diego lost the next week in temperatures that reached 59 degrees below zero (with the wind-chill factor) in Cincinnati, 1 game short of the Super Bowl. Incredibly, Fouts never played in a Super Bowl.

OPPOSITE: **Under Coach Don Coryell, Dan Fouts and the Chargers flourished on offense. The team's passing game was so strong that the Chargers were referred to as "Air Coryell."**

OTTO GRAHAM

BELOW: **Otto Graham, stepping lively in Converse hightops, eludes the Rams in the 1950 NFL Championship Game, won by the Cleveland Browns 30-28.** OPPOSITE: **In terms of efficiency and skill, Graham (scrambling for a touchdown against the Detroit Lions in 1954) was ahead of his time.**

Long before Joe Montana and Dan Marino started launching bombs in the 1980s, there was Otto Graham. He played for the Cleveland Browns from 1946 to 1955, in an era when passing fancy was considered risqué. Most passers in his day lacked finesse and threw as many interceptions as touchdowns. But Graham had an uncanny ability to guide his powerful spirals between defenders, into the hands of his receivers.

You can find him today in a position of eminence; he's history's fourth-rated passer (86.6), based on the complicated formula. There he is, ahead of such thoroughly modern passers as Jim Kelly, Troy Aikman, Roger Staubach, and Bart Starr. Graham is the only quarterback who played in the All-America Football Conference to be listed among history's twenty top-rated passers.

As often happened in his day, Graham began his football career as a running back. When he enrolled at Northwestern University, however, football was not in his plans. The six-foot-one-inch 195-pounder was a music major who played the violin and French horn.

Basketball was his forte, but he was discovered in a freshman intramural football game and played for three years at the varsity level.

Paul Brown, the great football mind, looked past Graham's accomplishments as a running back. He liked Graham's poise, his ball-handling abilities; he envisioned Graham as the perfect quarterback in his T-formation offense. When Brown started organizing the Cleveland Browns team for the new AAFC, his first signee was Graham. In his first two seasons, Graham led the league with 17 and 25 touchdown passes, respectively, balanced against a total of only 16 interceptions. In his four AAFC seasons, Graham was the leader in yards three times. He also ran regularly, played defense, and returned an occasional punt.

More importantly, Graham led the Browns to four championships in those four seasons. Cleveland produced an incredible 52-4-3 record, leading fans to wonder what the Browns could accomplish in the highly regarded National Football League. Graham silenced the skeptics by carrying the Browns to the NFL title game in 1950, throwing 4 touchdowns in the Browns' 30-28 victory over the Los Angeles Rams. Four years later, Graham scored 3 touchdowns on the ground and 3 more through the air in Cleveland's 56-10 razing of the Detroit Lions.

Graham, then thirty-three years old, elected to retire after that game but returned early in the 1955 season when summoned by a desperate Paul Brown. In the final game of his career, the championship against the Los Angeles Rams, Graham ran for 2 touchdowns and passed for 2 more in a 38-14 win that certified his greatness.

For the ninth time in ten seasons, Graham was named to the all-league team. And he left a legacy that no quarterback is likely to match. While he was handling the ball for the Browns, they appeared in 10 consecutive championship games, winning four AAFC titles and three NFL crowns.

DAN MARINO

Five quarterbacks were selected ahead of Daniel Constantine Marino in the 1983 draft, but when his glorious career is over, it is likely that his name will be first in the National Football League record book.

Heading into the 1995 season, Dan Marino held eighteen NFL passing records, and if his Achilles tear of 1993 doesn't trouble him, he should break the epic marks of Fran Tarkenton sometime in 1995 or 1996. Freak accidents aside, Marino should surpass Tarkenton's 6,467 passes attempted (Marino has 6,049), 3,686 passes completed (Marino has 3,604), 47,003 yards gained (Marino has 45,173), and 342 touchdowns (Marino has 328).

To put Marino's numbers in perspective, there is this comparison with Joe Montana, who is generally acknowledged to be the greatest quarterback of all time. After the 1993 season, after Montana's fifteenth year in the league, Marino's totals were all superior. And while Montana has history's second-best passer rating, Marino is third overall, behind Montana and San Francisco quarterback Steve Young.

"Dan Marino is the greatest drop-back passer ever," says no less an authority than the Miami Dolphins' Don Shula, the game's all-time winningest coach. (Remember, Shula also coached Hall of Fame quarterbacks Johnny Unitas and Bob Griese.) "From the beginning, he has had all the tools you could want: the physical skills, the toughness, the attitude."

And from the beginning, Marino has had luck riding on his magnificent right arm. Clearly he wouldn't have set all those records if he had wound up in Denver like John Elway, the first pick of the 1983 draft, or in Kansas City like Todd Blackledge. Rather, Marino slid all the way down to the draft's twenty-seventh overall pick, into the waiting arms of Shula. Thus, Marino the rookie had the rare privilege of playing for a team that had just been to the Super Bowl.

Marino started in 9 games in 1983 and threw 20 touchdowns and only 6 interceptions. He was named the Rookie of the Year and became the first rookie quarterback ever named to start in the Pro Bowl—a special honor, considering he was voted in by his playing peers. In 1984 Marino achieved an almost surreal level of efficiency. He finished the season with a staggering 48 touchdowns and 5,084 yards, standards that endure today as the NFL's best ever. One of every 8.5 pass attempts resulted in a score. As a frame of reference, consider that Marino broke Griese's team pass yardage record in the ninth game of the season. Marino torched the Pittsburgh Steelers for 421 yards and 4 touchdowns in the Dolphins' 45-28 victory in the AFC Championship Game. In the Super Bowl, the sophomore quarterback completed an impressive 29 of 50 passes for 318 yards, but Montana's San Francisco 49ers prevailed.

Marino didn't know it at the time, but that would be the only Super Bowl appearance for him through 1993. And as the numbers pile up into the 1990s, a Super Bowl ring remains the only meaningful hardware that Marino lacks.

"It doesn't haunt me that we haven't won the Super Bowl yet," Marino says. "But I think about it sometimes. It's everybody's dream. Every player in this league wants to win the Super Bowl, and I'm no different.

"It's something I've been doing my whole life since I was a little kid. I do it well. There's that feeling that you've worked all week and prepared and there's the excitement with the crowd that is just incredible. I still can't explain the feeling, even after all these years."

JOE MONTANA

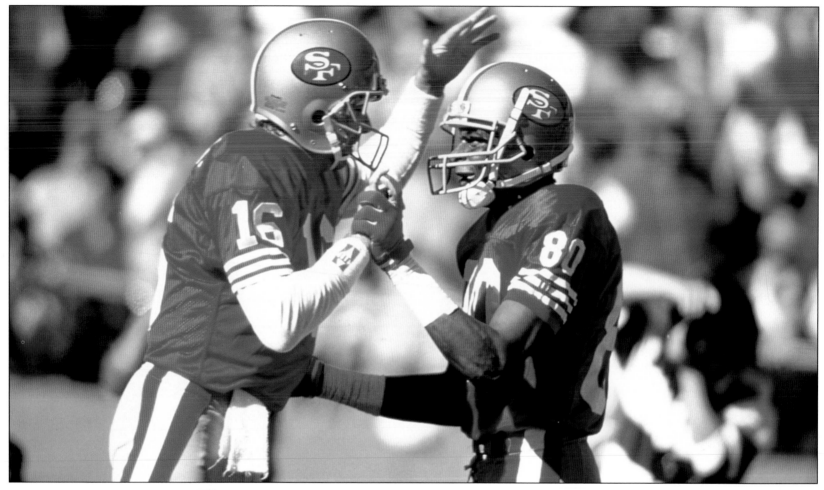

San Francisco's Joe Montana, here with his greatest collaborator, wide receiver Jerry Rice, is probably the best quarterback under pressure in the history of the game.

Bill Walsh, the former San Francisco 49ers coach, likes to tell a story about Joe Montana. It is training camp in 1979, Montana's rookie season. He stands at six feet two inches and weighs 195 pounds—not much to look at—and joins the 49ers as the fourth quarterback taken in the draft, after Jack Thompson, Phil Simms, and Steve Fuller.

Montana is sitting in the lobby of the Howard Johnson where the team housed its rookies. Wide receiver Dwight Clark, himself a rookie, laid his eyes on Montana, who was slight, spindly, and longhaired. Clark had read the press clippings lauding the heroic Notre Dame quarterback. "You're Joe Montana, the quarterback?" Clark asked, incredulous.

"He doesn't have the stature of a Marino or an Elway," Walsh says. "But he has all the intangibles you could want. When the game is on the line, he is the man you want to have the ball."

The 49ers appeared in four Super Bowls in nine seasons, and though there were two head coaches, three primary running backs, and three principal wide receivers in that span from 1981 to 1990, Montana was the constant. He was voted the Most Valuable Player in 3 of those games, and in the fourth—a thrilling 20-16 come-from-behind victory over Cincinnati—Montana moved the 49ers 92 yards to the winning score with 34 seconds left. In that game he completed 23 of 36 passes for a Super Bowl record of 357 yards and 2 touchdowns. Wide receiv-

Whether he was passing for the Kansas City Chiefs late in his career *(FAR LEFT)* or for the 49ers *(LEFT)*, Montana's presence in the pocket inspired his teammates, sometimes beyond their limitations.

er Jerry Rice was voted the MVP in that game, but each of his 11 catches came from the right hand of Montana.

It was an echo of Montana's first Super Bowl (XVI), played against Cincinnati in January 1982. In his third year, Montana completed 14 of 22 passes for 157 yards. That 26-21 win was possible only because Montana had thrown "The Catch" to Clark to beat the Dallas Cowboys in the NFC Championship Game.

Not only is Montana the quintessential clutch performer, he is technically the second most efficient quarterback. The NFL passer rating, which measures five statistics, places Montana as the second-best of all time. His rating heading into 1994 (93.1) edged Steve Young's (93.0) at the time and left the rest of the pack (Dan Marino was third, at 88.1) far behind.

In 1989, at the age of thirty-three, Montana had his best all-around season. He completed 271 of 386 passes (70.2 percent), for 3,521 yards, 26 touchdowns, and only 8 interceptions. It all added up to a passer rating of 112.4, breaking the record of Milt Plum, who produced a 110.4 in 1960. The 49ers, by now coached by George Seifert, won their fourth Super Bowl that season, eras-

ing Denver 55-10 in Super Bowl XXIV. Montana completed 22 of 29 passes for 297 yards and 5 touchdowns, a Super Bowl record.

Montana, despite his greatness, was never blessed with good health. He successfully underwent potentially career-ending back surgery in 1986, and was troubled with a chronically damaged elbow. He did not throw a pass in the 1991 season, and in 1992 he appeared in only 1 game for the 49ers. Before the 1993 season began, the 49ers had settled on Young as their starter and traded Montana to the Kansas City Chiefs.

Montana was thirty-seven years old when the 1993 season started and had thrown only 21 passes in the previous two seasons, but he finished the season as the AFC's second-best passer, behind Denver's John Elway. Troubled by a nagging hamstring injury, Montana completed 181 of 298 passes, to go with 13 touchdowns and 7 interceptions. The Chiefs made the playoffs, largely due to Montana. Montana had another good year in 1994, but in 1995 announced his retirement. The man many consider to be the greatest quarterback of all time had played his last season.

JOE NAMATH

Joe Namath was a charismatic quarterback with a knack for showmanship: his memorable pre–Super Bowl guarantee of victory in 1969 is part of pro sports legend.

You will find his name in the NFL record book only three times for regular-season accomplishments, placing him in the company of such performers as Arnie Herber, Rich Gannon, and Lynn Dickey. And, no, he is not listed among history's top-rated quarterbacks—not even close—but Joe Namath is in the Hall of Fame, and deservedly so.

Despite his slender build and, in later years, his ravaged knees, the six-foot-two-inch, 200-pound Namath was "the greatest athlete I ever coached," according to his college coach, Alabama's Bear Bryant. In Namath's last three seasons there, the Crimson Tide lost only 3 regular-season games. Namath's 1964 Orange Bowl performance against Texas convinced the professional scouts he was worthy.

Namath's powerful arm and lightning-quick release made him a coveted commodity in 1965, and the Los Angeles Rams of the National Football League and the New York Jets of the rival American Football League both drafted him in the first round. Namath spurned the established NFL for the Jets' record-setting $400,000 contract, lending instant credibility to the junior league.

Four seasons later, Namath was sitting at the pool deck of the Jets' Super Bowl hotel when he told reporters, "We are going to win the Super Bowl." He guaranteed it, and his hubris quickly made headlines around the country. Namath's words were considered ludicrous, because the Baltimore Colts were 17-point favorites in Super Bowl III. The two previous AFC champions, Kansas City and Oakland, had been humbled by the Green Bay Packers, and the 1969 Colts were 15-1.

The Jets managed only 2 first downs in the first quarter, but Namath moved New York 80 yards for a touchdown in the second quarter. Placekicker Jim Turner added 3 field goals in the second half and the Jets' defense held Baltimore to a single touchdown. The final score was 16-7; Namath had completed 17 of 28 passes for 206 yards. He was named the Most Valuable Player in one of the greatest championship upsets in league history. Suddenly, the AFL was seen on equal footing with the NFL. A year later, the two leagues merged into a twernty-six team entity that would captivate audiences in record numbers.

Namath produced impressive numbers throughout his career. He threw for more than 300 yards six times in 1967, four times in the Super Bowl season of 1968, and three times in 1969. In 1972 Namath cleared the 400-yard mark on two occasions. Against Baltimore that year, Namath had a career game: he threw for 496 yards and 6 touchdowns.

Despite his terminally weak knees, Namath did not miss a game because of injuries during the first five seasons of his career. But as time passed, Namath missed significant time with wrist, shoulder, and knee injuries. He wound up his career in 1977, with the Los Angeles Rams. His totals—3,762 attempts, 1,886 completions, 27,663 yards, and 173 touchdowns—are good but not great. But Namath's accomplishments transcend mere numbers; he saved an old league and helped create a stronger new one.

In Super Bowl III against the Baltimore Colts, Joe Namath personally laid the groundwork for the National Football League's merger with the American Football League. He completed 17 of 28 passes to lead the New York Jets to a stunning 16-7 victory.

BART STARR

OPPOSITE: **Starr led the Packers to victory in each of the first two Super Bowls and was named the Most Valuable Player both times. Here, he outruns the Oakland Raiders in Super Bowl II.**

RIGHT: **Bart Starr's statistics pale in comparison to today's pass-happy quarterbacks but he was the consummate winner in Green Bay. Here, Starr is about to launch the ball in Super Bowl I.**

Bart Starr played sixteen seasons in the National Football League, and his career totals, by today's air-assault standards, are modest. Boomer Esiason has a higher passer rating; Dave Krieg has more yards; Danny White has more touchdowns; and Neil Lomax, who played only eight seasons, has more completions. But in an eight-season span in Green Bay, Starr surpassed them all on the way to Canton, Ohio, and the Pro Football Hall of Fame.

Between 1960 and 1967, Starr led Vince Lombardi's Packers to five NFL championships, including the first two Super Bowls. The Packers' record in that time was a gaudy 82-24-4, and though Starr was overlooked by the public in favor of other star-quality players like Jim Taylor, Paul Hornung, and Ray Nitschke, Lombardi always maintained that his quarterback was the true star.

That Starr would emerge as one of the great quarterbacks of all time seemed unlikely following his college career. He had played at the University of Alabama, where the six-foot-one-inch 200-pounder played in the Orange Bowl as a freshman and then guided the Crimson Tide to victory the next season in the Cotton Bowl. But injuries left him on the bench most of his junior and senior seasons, and it wasn't until the seventeenth round of the 1956 draft that the Packers finally selected him. For three years in Green Bay, Starr did not have a hand in a single victory.

Starr's stock was low when Lombardi arrived in 1959, but the new coach liked Starr's ball-handling skills and marveled at the decisions he made at the line of scrimmage. Lombardi, carefully building Starr's confidence, eased him into the lineup. The quarterback won the last 4 games of the 1959 season and the

Packers finished above .500 for the first time in a dozen years. The next season, Green Bay was the Western Division champion, and Lombardi was moved to trade away veteran quarterback Lamar McHan. Starr's confidence soared.

The Packers went 11-3 in 1961 and won the NFL championship 37-0, over the New York Giants. Starr led the league in passing in 1962, 1964, and 1966. Not only did he make the big plays; he avoided the disastrous ones that hamstrung many quarterbacks and their teams. Over one span, from 1964 to 1965, Starr threw 294 consecutive passes without an interception—an NFL record until Cleveland's Bernie Kosar managed 308 from 1990 to 1991.

Green Bay won NFL titles in 1965 and 1966, and Starr was the MVP in the inaugural Super Bowl. He completed 16 of 23 passes for 250 yards and 2 touchdowns in a 35-10 victory over the Kansas City Chiefs.

The last championship under Lombardi may have been the most difficult to achieve. In a game where the temperature dipped to fifteen degrees below zero, Starr lifted the Packers over the Dallas Cowboys in the 1967 NFL Championship Game. Starr threw 2 touchdown passes to keep Green Bay in it; then, with 13 seconds left to play, he won the game with a typically shrewd call. Eschewing a field goal that would have tied the game at 17, Starr called his own number. He followed guard Jerry Kramer into the end zone for a 1-yard touchdown, giving the Packers a 21-17 win in the game that became known as "The Ice Bowl."

The subsequent 33-14 victory over the Oakland Raiders in Super Bowl II was anticlimactic. Starr was the MVP of that game, too, completing 13 of 24 passes for 202 yards. The Packers were 2-0 in the sport's ultimate game, but more importantly, they had won three consecutive NFL titles from 1965 to 1967, riding the right arm of Starr. None of the great teams that followed—the Dallas Cowboys, the Miami Dolphins, the Washington Redskins, and the San Francisco 49ers— ever matched that feat.

ROGER STAUBACH

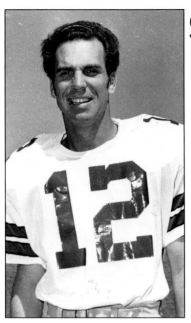

Sometimes, even the world of sports is visited by the specter of war. Hundreds of Major League Baseball players missed entire seasons as World War II dragged on; one can only wonder what kind of numbers Boston Red Sox slugger Ted Williams would have produced had he not missed the 1943, 1944, and 1945 seasons in the service of his country. What further records might boxer Muhammad Ali have set if he hadn't served time in jail for refusing to serve in the military? Likewise, how differently would football history read if Roger Staubach hadn't missed four seasons because of his commitments to the navy?

The six-foot-three-inch, 202-pound quarterback arrived at the United States Naval Academy in 1961, and two years later Navy went 9-1 with the scrambling Staubach taking snaps under center. Staubach won the 1963 Heisman Trophy, which goes to the nation's best player. The Dallas Cowboys of the National Football League and the Kansas City Chiefs of the American Football League both drafted Staubach as a future selection, aware that he had another year at Annapolis before graduation and a possible stint in the navy. The Cowboys, who offered an attractive signing bonus, plus continuing payments during his navy tenure, won out. But it wasn't until 1969 that Staubach, by then twenty-seven years old, finally pulled on a Dallas uniform for the first time.

For the Cowboys, it would prove well worth the wait. When Staubach first arrived, the charismatic Don Meredith had retired and the starter's job had been filled by veteran Craig Morton. Staubach started in only 2 games in each of his first two seasons, the second season ending in a dramatic 16-13 Super Bowl V loss—with Morton at the helm—to the Baltimore Colts. But 7 games into the 1971 season, with a middling record of 4-3, Landry moved Staubach ahead of Morton on the depth chart. The Cowboys did not lose another game all season long. There were 7 straight wins to end the regular season, followed by playoff victories over Minnesota and San Francisco. Staubach completed 12 of 19 passes for 119 yards and 2 touchdowns in a 24-3 win over the Miami Dolphins in Super Bowl VI.

In his first full season, the twenty-nine-year-old Staubach led the NFL in passing, a feat he would match in 1973, 1978, and 1979. In the nine seasons that Staubach was the starter, the Cowboys won 85 games and lost only 30, for an incandescent winning percentage of .739. Staubach led Dallas to the postseason eight times in that span, failing to reach the playoffs only in the injury-plagued 1974 season. Staubach was also the winning quarterback in Super Bowl XXII, a 27-10 victory over the Denver Broncos.

His final numbers, compiled in only eleven seasons, were impressive. Staubach completed 1,685 of 2,958 passes for 22,700 yards and 153 touchdowns. When he retired in 1979, his passer rating of 83.4 was history's best; even today it ranks as the league's sixth-best figure.

But beyond the bare numbers was Staubach's ability to bring the Cowboys back from the verge of defeat. On twenty-three occasions, Staubach rallied Dallas in the fourth quarter. Fourteen of those comebacks occurred in the game's final two minutes or overtime.

"He was," says Landry, "the greatest competitor I ever coached."

OPPOSITE: After a tour of duty in the navy, Staubach didn't play his first full season until he reached the age of twenty-nine. He went on to distinguish himself in eleven seasons and wound up in the Pro Football Hall of Fame. Here, he scans the field during Super Bowl VI, which the Cowboys won in convincing fashion.

FRAN TARKENTON

In today's National Football League, Fran Tarkenton would never have been allowed to play the game. He was, in short, a throwback to a time when quarterbacks were average-size players with extraordinary running ability and modest passing skills. Tarkenton was listed at six feet and 185 pounds in the program, but in truth he stood barely five feet ten inches. Unlike the prototypical six-foot-three-inch pocket passers, Tarkenton would leave the safety of the pocket at the slightest provocation. Critics wondered if he would live through a single game, much less an entire season.

And yet, Tarkenton survived eighteen seasons in the NFL and compiled a staggering set of numbers that has withstood assaults by such modern quarterbacks as Joe Montana, Dan Marino, and John Elway (as of 1994). You can find Tarkenton's name at the top of the list in the quarterback's four bottom-line categories: attempts (6,467), completions (3,686), yards (47,003), and touchdowns (342). No one has been more prolific, though Marino is likely to surpass Tarkenton's records one day.

It was typical of Tarkenton's muted reception in the NFL that the league's all-time leading quarterback was not the first draft choice out of college in 1961. The Minnesota Vikings, in their first-ever draft, chose Tulane running back Tommy Mason with the first overall pick, then took North Carolina linebacker Rip Hawkins in the second round. Tarkenton, who led the nation with a completion percentage of 58.4 as a senior at the University of Georgia, was the third-round choice.

In the franchise's first game, however, Tarkenton had a debut of historic proportions. Tarkenton came off the bench in relief of veteran George Shaw to pass for 250 yards and 4 touchdowns. He ran for a fifth touchdown in a 37-13 upset of the Chicago Bears and never stopped scrambling. Tarkenton played in

OPPOSITE: Tarkenton was small by today's quarterback standards, but he posed a big problem for his opponents with his scrambling ability; an opposing defense that overplayed its pass-rushing hand was often burned when he scrambled out of the pocket.

FAR LEFT: When he retired in 1979, Tarkenton was the NFL's all-time leader in yards, attempts, and completions.

LEFT: Tarkenton was a gritty competitor with an array of offensive weapons.

Minnesota for six seasons, then moved to the New York Giants from 1967 to 1971 (in a trade that cost the Giants two first-round and two second-round choices) before returning to the Vikings from 1972 to 1978.

Tarkenton's scrambling, never-give-in style was his signature. His ability to ad-lib under duress was unmatched. In one play late in his career, Tarkenton scrambled for twenty-eight seconds before locating wide receiver Sammy Smith and reaching him with a 45-yard touchdown pass. Incredibly, Tarkenton's career rushing total of 3,674 yards is better than six modern-era Hall of Fame running backs. Tarkenton's seemingly reckless approach did not abbreviate his career as some had thought it might. He didn't miss a game until 1976, when bruised ribs forced him to the sidelines.

And while Tarkenton was clearly a winner in terms of both team and individual records, one great prize always eluded him. He was playing in New York when the Vikings made their first Super Bowl appearance at the end of the 1969 season. And on his return to the Vikings, he guided Minnesota to three Super Bowls in a span of four years—all losses to superior American Football Conference teams. At the age of thirty-eight, Tarkenton played the 1978 season with the sole goal of winning a Super Bowl. And although he registered personal bests with 345 completions, 3,468 yards, and 25 touchdowns, Tarkenton could not prevent a playoff loss to the Rams. He retired without a Super Bowl ring in 1979, but could be comforted with the fact that no quarterback in history has done more for his teams.

JOHNNY UNITAS

Johnny Unitas crosses the goal line just ahead of two New York Giants defenders in the 1959 NFL Championship Game. The Baltiore Colts were 31-16 winners.

If reaching the end zone is football's bottom line, then Johnny Unitas is at the top of the heap when it comes to quarterbacks. In 47 consecutive games (49, including the 1958 and 1959 National Football League Championship Games) between 1956 and 1960, Unitas threw at least 1 touchdown pass, a record that conceivably could last forever. Consider that the Miami Dolphins' Dan Marino is second, with a 30-game streak.

From 1957 to 1960 Unitas led the NFL in touchdown passes. And although the Baltimore Colts' quarterback's totals of 24, 19, 32, and 25 seem rather modest by today's inflationary standards, no quarterback in league history ever led in that critical category four seasons running. Len Dawson needed five seasons and two teams in two different leagues—the Kansas City Chiefs and Dallas Texans—to do it. Marino, who one day will likely own most important passing records, could only manage three straight touchdown titles, from 1984 to 1986.

When the Pro Football Hall of Fame board of selectors was asked in 1969 to name an all-time quarterback from the NFL's first fifty years, it is small wonder that Unitas was the choice. And even as Marino, Joe Montana, and John Elway pass on their way toward the Hall of Fame, some of the old-time purists will argue that Unitas remains the greatest quarterback ever.

Incredibly, he almost never had the chance to display his prowess under center. A ninth-round draft choice of the Pittsburgh Steelers in 1955, Unitas was cut without throwing a pass in any meaningful game. Colts coach Weeb Ewbank, who was looking for a backup to starter George Shaw, signed Unitas to a modest contract in 1956. The six-foot-one-inch, 195-pound player entered the fourth game of the season when Shaw was injured; Unitas' first NFL pass was intercepted by Chicago and returned for a touchdown. Unitas finished his rookie season with 9 touchdown passes and 10 interceptions, a credible first-year ratio.

As the Colts' regular starter in 1957, Unitas led the league in attempts (301), yards (2,550), and touchdowns (27). Baltimore improved from 5-7 in 1956 to 7-5 in

1957. The breakthrough came in 1958, when the Colts won the Western Conference with a 9-3 record. When the New York Giants won the Eastern Conference with a 10-0 playoff victory, the stage was set for the most important game in NFL history.

At that time, baseball was still the national pastime and football was an afterthought—until the Giants and Colts waged their epic battle on national television. Baltimore led 14-3 in the first half, thanks largely to Unitas' 15-yard touchdown pass to Raymond Berry. Then the Giants took a 17-14 lead late in the game. With two minutes left, the Colts began a drive on their own

14 yard line. Unitas threw 7 straight passes, 4 of them complete and 3 to Berry. Steve Myrha's field goal—made with seven seconds remaining in regulation—sent the game into overtime. Unitas drove the Colts 80 yards to the winning touchdown, a 1-yard plunge by running back Alan Ameche, giving Baltimore the 23-17 victory.

Historians argue that this game was the catalyst in American sports fans' rush to embrace football. It also solidified Unitas' credentials as a poised leader under pressure. In 1973, after eighteen seasons, Unitas retired as the league's all-time leader (at the time) in touchdowns (290) and yards (40,239).

Unitas bridged the gap of the gritty, old-style offenses of the NFL and the pass-heavy offenses of the modern era. In Super Bowl III, he played opposite the New York Jets and brash Joe Namath.

NORM VAN BROCKLIN

National Football League games have been played since 1920, but no one has ever had a day quite like the one Norm Van Brocklin had on September 28, 1951. The Los Angeles Rams' quarterback threw for a dizzying 554 yards against the New York Yankees— an NFL record that stands today, against all odds. The best efforts of modern gunslingers Dan Marino of the Miami Dolphins (521 yards in 1988) and Warren Moon (527 yards in 1990, as a member of the Houston Oilers) weren't good enough to top Van Brocklin in the record book.

Ironically, Van Brocklin, one of football's most colorful players, wasn't even the Rams' full-time starter that year. The Rams drafted him in 1949, a year early out of the University of Oregon. Van Brocklin, a consensus All-America, opted to forego his final year of eligibility, but there was a problem in Los Angeles: Rams coach Clark Shaughnessy already had a future Hall of Fame quarterback in Bob Waterfield. In his only significant action as a rookie, the six-foot-one-inch, 190-pound Van Brocklin fired 4 touchdown passes against the Washington Redskins to give the Rams the Western Division title.

When new coach Joe Stydahar saw Van Brocklin's obvious skill in practice, he devised a rotation system that featured Waterfield in the first and third quarters and Van Brocklin in the second and fourth quarters. Neither player liked the compromise, but the results were indisputable. Van Brocklin won the 1950 passing title, completing 127 of 233 passes for 2,061 yards and 18 touchdowns. Waterfield won the 1951 passing championship, edging out Van Brocklin in the season's final game.

The Rams finished the regular season that year with an 8-4 record and faced heavily favored Cleveland (11-1) in the NFL Championship Game.

With Waterfield calling the signals, the Rams found themselves in a surprising 17-point tie midway through the fourth quarter. Following his intuition, Stydahar called Van Brocklin off the bench and "The Dutchman" threw a 73-yard touchdown pass that eventually gave the Rams a 24-17 victory over the defending league champions.

In 1952 Van Brocklin returned as the league's best passer, which sent Waterfield into retirement. Van Brocklin was also the league's best passer in 1954. Van Brocklin was traded to the Philadelphia Eagles in 1958, where two years later he enjoyed his most satisfying season.

The Eagles finished second in 1959, and in 1960 they reached the league championship. Led by Van Brocklin, the Eagles became the first and only team to defeat Green Bay Packers coach Vince Lombardi in a title game, winning 17-13. At the age of thirty-four, Van Brocklin was the league's Most Valuable Player and finished his twelve-year career in his eighth Pro Bowl. He went out in typical incendiary fashion: Van Brocklin threw touchdown passes of 46, 43, and 36 yards, then completed 6 straight passes in an attempt to salvage what had looked to be a hopeless game.

It was that final season that landed Van Brocklin in the Pro Football Hall of Fame more than a decade later, in 1971.

Van Brocklin left the field after 1960 to become head coach of the fledgling Minnesota Vikings. The record that first year was a difficult 3-11, and Van Brocklin's six-year mark in Minnesota was 29-51-4. Two years after he left the Vikings, Van Brocklin surfaced as the coach of the Atlanta Falcons. His seven-year record there was a middling 37-49-3, but in no way could his coaching diminish his constributions on the field.

In twelve seasons, the gifted Norm Van Brocklin was voted to appear in the Pro Bowl eight times.

STEVE YOUNG

Early in his San Francisco career, Young was known primarily as a quarterback who preferred to run first and pass later. As he showed in the drubbing of the Chargers in Super Bowl XXIX, Young now poses a double threat, being both an agile, versatile scrambler and an incredible passer.

Until the 1994 season, the curse of being Steve Young was that only one quarterback in the history of the National Football League had posted a better career passer rating: Joe Montana. And then Young exorcised the ghost of No. 16 with an unprecedented season. He completed 324 of 461 passes for 3,969 yards and 35 touchdowns. Young's passer rating was a staggering 112.8, breaking Montana's single-season record.

Young was named the league's Most Valuable Player for the second time in three years and the 49ers won the Super Bowl with ease over the San Diego Chargers. Young threw for a record 6 touchdowns.

In 1993 Young achieved something that Montana—and every other quarterback, for that matter—had not. Young completed 314 of 462 passes for 4,023 yards, 29 touchdowns, and 16 interceptions for the 49ers. His passer rating of 101.5 edged the 99.0 of Dallas Cowboys quarterback Troy Aikman and gave Young an unprecedented third consecutive passing title. Montana never even put together back-to-back passing titles.

This was just the sort of performance that former 49ers head coach Bill Walsh envisioned when he traded for Young in 1987. After Young signed a record forty-million-dollar contract with the L.A. Express and played two seasons in the now-defunct United States Football League and then two years with the Tampa Bay Buccaneers, Walsh sent a second-round and a fourth-round draft choice to the Bucs for the rights to the quarterback.

Young saw little action until age began to catch up with Montana. Young played in 11 games in 1991, when Montana was sidelined with an elbow injury, and produced a rating of 101.8. In a full 16-game schedule in 1992, Young completed 268 of 402 passes (for a completion percentage of 66.7), throwing for 3,465 yards, 25 touchdowns, and only 7 interceptions. After a phenomenal 1993 season, Young produced a 100 rating three years in a row. For perspective, consider that a rating of 100 has been recorded only fourteen other times in history. Naturally, Montana is the only other man with three such seasons.

In terms of style, Young was nearly the antithesis of Montana. While most quarterbacks, including Montana, are right-handed, Young is left-handed. There is also Young's running ability. Some scouts maintain to this day that Young, at six feet two inches and 200 pounds, could achieve success as a running back. In 1988 he scrambled 49 yards for an unbelievable touchdown against the Minnesota Vikings in which he broke 7 tackles. But as Young settled into the celebrated 49ers offense, a legacy of Walsh, he ran less and passed more. And the numbers mounted.

The 49ers drew criticism in 1993 when they dealt the thirty-seven-year-old Montana to Kansas City. And even when Young posted terrific numbers, people couldn't help but wonder why San Francisco hadn't been to the Super Bowl in three years of Young's stewardship. Young's magnificent performance in Super Bowl XXIX silenced the critics forever.

Steve Young and the 49ers thrashed the defending champion Cowboys in the 1994 NFC Championship Game.

APPENDIX: QUARTERBACK STATISTICS

Player	Year	Att.	Comp.	Yards	Pct.	TD	Int.
Troy Aikman	1989	293	155	1,749	52.9	9	18
	1990	399	226	2,579	56.6	11	18
	1991	363	237	2,754	65.3	11	10
	1992	473	302	3,445	63.8	23	14
	1993	392	271	3,100	69.1	15	6
	1994	361	233	2,676	64.5	13	12
Sammy Baugh	1937	171	81	1,127	47.4	7	14
	1938	128	63	853	49.2	5	11
	1939	96	53	518	55.2	6	9
	1940	177	111	1,367	62.7	12	10
	1941	193	106	1,236	54.9	10	19
	1942	225	132	1,524	58.7	16	11
	1943	239	133	1,754	55.6	23	19
	1944	146	82	849	56.2	4	8
	1945	182	128	1,669	70.3	11	4
	1946	161	87	1,163	54.0	8	17
	1947	354	210	2,938	59.3	25	15
	1948	315	185	2,599	58.7	22	23
	1949	255	145	1,903	56.9	18	14
	1950	166	90	1,130	54.2	10	11
	1951	154	67	1,104	43.5	7	17
	1952	33	20	152	60.6	2	1
Terry Bradshaw	1970	218	83	1,410	38.1	6	24
	1971	373	302	2,259	54.4	13	22
	1972	308	147	1,887	47.7	12	12
	1973	180	89	1,183	49.4	10	15
	1974	148	67	785	45.3	7	8
	1975	286	165	2,055	57.7	18	9
	1976	192	92	1,177	47.9	10	9
	1977	314	162	2,523	51.6	17	19
	1978	368	207	2,915	56.3	28	20
	1979	472	259	3,724	54.9	26	25
	1980	424	218	3,339	51.4	24	22
	1981	370	201	2,887	54.3	22	14
	1982	240	127	1,768	52.9	17	11
	1983	8	5	77	62.5	2	0
John Elway	1983	259	123	1,663	47.5	7	14
	1984	380	214	2,598	56.3	18	15
	1985	605	327	3,891	54.0	22	23

Player	Year	Att.	Comp.	Yards	Pct.	TD	Int.
	1986	504	280	3,485	55.6	19	13
	1987	410	224	3,198	54.6	19	12
	1988	496	274	3,309	55.2	17	19
	1989	416	223	3.051	53.6	18	18
	1990	502	294	3,526	58.6	15	14
	1991	451	242	3,253	53.7	13	12
	1992	316	174	2,242	55.1	10	17
	1993	551	348	4,030	63.2	25	10
	1994	493	307	3,490	62.1	16	10
Dan Fouts	1973	194	87	1,126	44.8	6	13
	1974	237	115	1,732	48.5	8	13
	1975	195	106	1,395	54.4	2	10
	1976	359	208	2,535	57.9	14	15
	1977	109	69	869	63.3	4	6
	1978	381	224	2,999	58.8	24	20
	1979	530	332	4,082	62.6	24	24
	1980	589	348	4,715	59.1	30	24
	1981	609	360	4,802	59.1	33	17
	1982	330	204	2,883	61.8	17	11
	1983	340	215	2,975	63.2	20	15
	1984	507	317	3,740	62.5	19	17
	1985	430	254	3,638	59.1	27	20
	1986	430	252	3,031	58.6	16	22
	1987	364	206	2,517	56.6	10	15
Otto Graham	1946*	174	95	1,834	54.6	17	5
	1947*	269	163	2,753	60.6	25	11
	1948*	333	173	2,713	52.0	25	15
	1949*	285	161	2,785	56.5	19	10
	1950	253	137	1,943	54.2	14	20
	1951	264	147	2,205	55.5	17	16
	1952	364	181	2,816	49.7	20	24
	1953	258	167	2,722	64.7	11	9
	1954	240	142	2,092	59.2	11	17
	1955	185	98	1,721	53.0	15	8
Dan Marino	1983	296	173	2,210	58.4	20	6
	1984	564	362	5,084	64.2	48	17
	1985	567	336	4,137	59.3	30	21
	1986	623	378	4,746	60.7	44	23
	1987	444	263	3,245	59.2	26	13

Player	Year	Att.	Comp.	Yards	Pct.	TD	Int.	Player	Year	Att.	Comp.	Yards	Pct.	TD	Int.
	1988	606	354	4,434	58.4	28	23		1962	285	178	2,438	62.5	12	9
	1989	550	308	3,997	56.0	24	22		1963	244	132	1,855	54.1	15	10
	1990	531	306	3,563	57.6	21	11		1964	272	163	2,144	59.9	15	4
	1991	549	318	3,970	57.9	25	13		1965	251	140	2,055	55.8	16	9
	1992	554	330	4,116	59.6	24	16		1966	251	156	2,257	62.2	14	3
	1993	150	91	1,218	60.7	8	3		1967	210	115	1,823	54.8	9	17
	1994	615	385	4,453	62.6	30	17		1968	171	109	1,617	63.7	15	8
									1969	118	92	1,161	62.2	9	6
Joe Montana	1979	23	13	96	56.5	1	0		1970	255	140	1,645	54.9	8	13
	1980	273	176	1,795	64.5	15	9		1971	45	24	286	53.3	0	3
	1981	488	311	3,565	63.7	19	12								
	1982	346	213	2,613	61.6	17	11	Roger Staubach	1969	47	23	421	48.9	1	2
	1983	515	332	3,910	64.5	26	12		1970	82	44	542	53.7	2	8
	1984	432	279	3,630	64.6	28	10		1971	211	126	1,882	59.7	15	4
	1985	494	303	3,653	61.3	27	13		1972	20	9	98	45.0	0	2
	1986	307	191	2,236	62.2	8	9		1973	286	179	2,428	62.6	23	15
	1987	398	266	3,054	66.8	31	13		1974	360	190	2,552	52.8	11	15
	1988	397	238	2,981	59.9	18	10		1975	348	198	2,666	56.9	17	16
	1989	386	271	3,521	70.2	26	8		1976	369	208	2,715	56.4	14	11
	1990	520	321	3,944	61.7	26	16		1977	361	210	2,620	58.2	18	9
	1991‡	—	—	—	—	—	—		1978	413	231	3,190	55.9	25	16
	1992	21	15	126	71.4	2	0		1979	461	267	3,586	57.9	27	11
	1993	298	181	2,144	60.7	13	7								
	1994	493	299	3,283	60.6	16	9	Fran Tarkenton	1961	280	157	1,997	56.1	18	17
									1962	329	163	2,595	49.5	22	25
Joe Namath	1965	340	164	2,220	48.2	18	15		1963	297	170	2,311	57.2	15	15
	1966	471	232	3,379	49.3	19	27		1964	306	171	2,506	55.9	22	11
	1967	491	258	4,007	52.5	26	28		1965	329	171	2,609	52.0	19	11
	1968	380	187	3,147	49.2	15	17		1966	358	192	2,561	53.6	17	16
	1969	361	185	2,734	51.2	19	17		1967	377	204	3,088	54.1	29	19
	1970	179	90	1,259	50.3	5	12		1968	337	182	2,555	54.0	21	12
	1971	59	28	537	47.5	5	6		1969	409	220	2,918	53.8	23	8
	1972	324	162	2,816	50.0	19	21		1970	389	219	2,777	56.3	19	12
	1973	133	68	966	51.1	5	6		1971	386	226	2,567	58.5	11	21
	1974	361	191	2,616	52.9	20	22		1972	378	215	2,651	56.9	18	13
	1975	326	157	2,286	48.2	15	28		1973	274	169	2,113	61.7	15	7
	1976	230	114	1,090	49.6	4	16		1974	351	199	2,598	56.7	17	12
	1977	107	50	606	46.7	3	5		1975	425	273	2,994	64.2	25	13
									1976	412	255	2,961	61.9	17	8
Bart Starr	1956	44	24	325	54.5	2	3		1977	258	155	1,734	60.1	9	14
	1957	215	117	1,489	54.4	8	10		1978	572	345	3,468	60.3	25	32
	1958	157	78	875	49.7	3	12								
	1959	134	70	972	52.2	6	7	Johnny Unitas	1956	198	110	1,498	55.6	9	10
	1960	172	98	1,358	57.0	4	8		1957	301	172	2,550	57.1	24	17
	1961	295	172	2,418	58.3	16	16		1958	263	136	2,007	51.7	19	7

Player	Year	Att.	Comp.	Yards	Pct.	TD	Int.	Player	Year	Att.	Comp.	Yards	Pct.	TD	Int.
									1953	286	156	2,393	54.5	19	14
	1959	367	193	2,899	52.6	32	14		1954	260	139	2,637	53.5	13	21
	1960	378	190	3,099	50.3	25	24		1955	272	144	1,890	52.9	8	15
	1961	420	229	2,990	54.5	16	24		1956	124	68	966	54.8	7	12
	1962	389	222	2,967	57.1	23	23		1957	265	132	2,105	49.8	20	21
	1963	410	237	3,481	57.8	20	12		1958	374	198	2,409	52.9	15	20
	1964	305	158	2,824	51.8	19	6		1959	340	191	2,617	56.2	16	14
	1965	282	164	2,530	58.2	23	12		1960	284	153	2,471	53.9	24	17
	1966	348	195	2,743	56.0	22	24								
	1967	436	255	3,428	58.5	20	16	Steve Young	1984†	310	179	2,361	57.7	10	9
	1968	32	11	139	34.4	2	4		1985†	250	137	1,741	54.8	6	13
	1969	327	178	2,342	54.4	12	20		1985	138	72	935	52.2	3	8
	1970	321	166	2,213	51.7	14	18		1986	363	195	2,282	53.7	8	13
	1971	176	92	942	52.3	3	9		1987	69	37	570	53.6	10	0
	1972	157	88	1,111	56.1	4	6		1988	101	54	680	53.5	3	3
	1973	76	34	471	44.7	3	7		1989	92	64	1001	69.6	8	3
									1990	62	38	427	61.3	2	0
N. Van Brocklin	1949	58	32	601	55.2	6	2		1991	279	180	2,517	64.5	17	8
	1950	233	127	2,061	54.5	18	14		1992	402	268	3,465	66.7	25	7
	1951	194	100	1,725	51.5	13	11		1993	462	314	4,023	68.0	29	16
	1952	205	113	1,736	55.1	14	17		1994	461	324	3,969	70.3	35	10

* with the AAFC † with the USFL ‡ did not play

PHOTOGRAPHY CREDITS

© Allsport USA: 22; Rich Clarkson: 64 bottom; Chris Covatta: 21; Scott Cunningham: 68; Jonathan Daniel: 58; Stephen Dunn: 15, 47, 61 left; Otto Gruele: 13, 25 right; Jim Gund: 45; Bill Hickey: 30; Doug Pensinger: 59; Mike Powell: 5, 29, 44, 54, 61 right, 74, 75; Rick Stewart: 8, 10, 17 right, 31, 32

AP/Wide World Photos: 12 right, 19, 28, 36, 41, 49, 53, 55, 57, 63, 67, 70 bottom, 73

© Focus on Sports: 2, 40 right, 50 both, 65, 66, 69 right; © Mickey Palmer: 40 center, 51

Reuters/Bettmann: 37, 43

© Fred Roe: 11, 23

© Dan Rubin: 69 left

© Sportschrome East/West: 20; © Brian Drake: 27; © Steven Goldstein: 35

Sports Photo Masters, Inc.: © Jeff Carlick: 14, 60; © Mitchell B. Reibel: 24-25, 38, 40 left, 46, 52, 62

© Dave Stock: 6, 9, 16-17, 18, 26

UPI/Bettmann: 12 left, 48, 56 both, 64 top, 70 top, 71

INDEX